T0386637

γιαγια

γιαγια

TIME-PERFECTED RECIPES FROM GREECE'S GRANDMOTHERS

Anastasia Miari

Hardie Grant

BOOKS

This book is for my mum, who's about to become a grandmother herself.

For my daughter, who for an entire summer in utero, has been fed by the women that make up the pages of this book. I hope she'll continue to nourish herself with the same dishes, well into old age.

For Theia Poppy from Argyrades, who was the ultimate Greek yiayia, dressed in black and waiting on her white-washed stoop for me to come by so she could bless me and wish me as much happiness 'as the number of hairs on my head'. She should have been in this book.

And for Yiayia. Of course.

CONTENTS

PREFACE

This book has been a whirlwind in the making. In the same week that my very understanding editors at Hardie Grant commissioned *Yiayia*, I also found out I was pregnant. Cue an intense four-month odyssey across Greece, in which Marco Arguello (the brilliant photographer behind the evocative imagery in this book) and I barely saw our respective partners.

Along with a peppering of other ingredients, the journey I've been on to write this book is what makes this collection of recipes, stories and photography so special. These grandmothers welcomed Marco and I into their homes and were kind enough to show me first-hand how their time-perfected dishes were made.

While each yiayia cooked with me, letting me into her memories, with nostalgia often triggered by the aromas of the kitchen, Marco took to snooping around (no one ever seemed to mind!), snapping away at 'holy' corners packed with iconography or pattern-on-pattern kitchens that have miraculously escaped the passing of time.

Of course, I could have researched these recipes remotely, but it felt imperative to meet the women in person. Nothing in this book has been photographed in a studio setting. We were at the mercy of each yiayia's timings (and Greek yiayiades can rarely be pinned down or wrestled into a schedule) and of the weather (we chose perhaps the wettest week to shoot in Corfu and Marco still somehow managed to find a way to capture these women in their best light). Yiayia Despina in Symi was even kind enough to gift us her plastic tablecloth after seeing we'd taken a liking to it, using it as a filter for the harsh midday sun.

Along with the recipes I picked up on my travels, this book also includes recipes from some of my favourite Greeks working in food, along with a special dedication to their own yiayia. It is extra special that I have been able to include their cherished food memories within these pages. Reading some of them has brought more than just a single tear to the eye.

On the road, as we travelled from the Italian-influenced Ionian Islands to Balkan villages in the hills and wild, far-flung Cycladic islands, I bemoaned the fact that my daughter won't have a Greek yiayia. My own mother is English and my man's is Italian. Marco pointed out that while that may be true, over the course of one summer in the womb, she's been nourished by an entire nation of yiayiades. As I write this, I can't help but think about how lucky she already is, to be inheriting a tome of life lessons and recipes from Greece's greatest matriarchs in the pages of this book.

THE GREEK MATRIARCH

Yiayia was my first word.

Greek for 'grandmother', it has a harsher sound, which suits my own Greek grandmother down to the ground. Like many Greek yiayiades, my own is not a cutesy, cuddly granny sat at home doing the knitting. She's a grafter; a hardened woman who came of age during the post-war years in which most of Greece was still in poverty and experiencing civil unrest. 'Grandmother' seems too soft of a word to use for my gutsy yiayia, who savagely pulls the innards out of fish and slops them aggressively into the bowl she's working with, is prone to angry outbursts and still sweats over an open flame to prepare a meal.

In my most formative years, Yiayia took on the role of chief care provider while my parents worked. This meant accompanying her to fertile, muddy fields and watching her thwack the ground with a hoe before planting tomato seeds that would grow into giant red baubles come June. Or heading out into Corfu's torrential rain in October to pick olives from wizened old trees that weren't at all dissimilar to Yiayia's lined, weather-beaten face. I once watched her kill a snake right in front of me. It slinked its way through overgrown weeds towards me but before I'd even had a chance to cry out, Yiayia had sprung into action. She picked up an axe and swung at it fearlessly until the snake was just a writhing, wriggling tail.

In Greece there's a saying: Του παιδιού μου το παιδί, δυο φορές το γεννησα. *My own child's child, is mine twice over.*

My crude translation doesn't do it justice, but the general gist is that grandparents here see themselves as parents twice over. In my case, Yiayia was another maternal figure. This book is an obvious dedication to her but also to the women in Greece like her. Though they might not all be yiayiades in the sense that they have grandchildren, they are a breed of powerful matriarchs. They have the will to get up every morning – in spite of illness, loneliness and the complaints of old age – and cook themselves a dish from scratch, purely for the sake of giving themselves the pleasure that only a home-cooked meal can give.

They took care of the finances at home and raised families while their husbands were off fighting wars, working on cargo ships to send money home or else just off with other women. In an unashamedly patriarchal society, it is our yiayiades that have come off the strongest and that have, more often than not, lived the longest. Despite the sometimes awful hypocrisy they've had to face in life, these women are still here, they are alive and they are spirited. This book is a distillation of their lives and experiences, in the form of anecdotes and regional recipes that make up the complex and compelling tapestry of this country I call home.

I'm fully aware that the grandmothers of our world are not in short supply, but this specific breed – the Greek yiayia – won't be around in a couple of decades. At least, not in the sense that I have known them; dressed in mourning black, sat behind beaded curtains in white-washed houses, hunched over in fields foraging *horta* (wild greens) or waiting patiently for a *briki* (small saucepan for making coffee) to brew a rich, silty coffee. The generation succeeding my yiayia's drive their own cars, have jobs, get manicures and make *pites* (pies) with ready-made filo pastry bought from the supermarket.

In my village in Corfu, you can still spot the odd yiayia walking back from her allotment, *mantili* (headscarf) wrapped around her head, atop of which is perched a basket of produce, balanced with the precision and expertise of a street performer. These are the peers of my Yiayia Anastasia, the last generation of women in black that hold the secrets to living off the land and cooking the regional dishes that say more about Greece than any history book can.

This is my ode to them and to the great food of Greece.

REGIONS OF GREECE

Greek food is so much more than moussaka. Stuffed courgettes (zucchini) from Lesvos (see page 98), Cycladic *fourtalia* (Egg and Potato Omelette; see page 100), Corfiot *bourdeto* (Spicy Fish Stew; see pages 168–9), Cretan *dakos* (Barley Rusk Salad; see page 94) … If you don't know them now, you will once you start to leaf through the pages of this book.

Despite its popularity, what people know of Greek cuisine is still fairly limited when considering the breadth and diversity of dishes you can find in homes across our 6,000 islands and far-too-often-overlooked mainland. In this book, I'm delving into my own culinary heritage, exploring Greek cuisine through the matriarchs that know it best – the emphasis being on the Greek women putting the tastiest food on the table, each yiayia flavouring her time-perfected dish with her heritage.

On this journey, I've been surprised by the amount of pasta I encountered. Even in remote mountain villages far from the shores of Italy, home-rolled pasta is a staple. The same goes for the number of vegetables that can be stuffed. I've found that the golden rule is: if it's a vegetable, you can fill it with rice. The likely origin of that dish is much further east than Greece's modern borders.

In visiting the homes, *kafeneions* and tavernas of these matriarchs, I've managed to piece together a kind of culinary map of the nation.* From the kitchens of Corfu, packed with the flavours of Italy, it spreads through to the hearty dishes of Balkan-bordered mainland Greece and on to the light, bright, punchy summer recipes of the Cycladic and Aegean islands, influenced also by Turkey and its proximity to the eastern isles.

The Ionian Islands

Thanks to the Ionian Islands' proximity to Italy and Corfu having been under Venetian rule for 400 years, the Corfiot kitchen features dishes that are distinct in all of Greece. Pasta features heavily in our diets on Corfu (see pages 150 and 174–5), as do heavy additions of spice (to be accredited to the Venetians for putting the island on the spice trail), which feature in stews like bourdeto (*brodeto* in Italian), *stifado* (or *stufato*) and *pastitsada*. We can also tip our hats to the Italians for *pasta frolla* shortcrust pastry tarts (see page 242–3), much of our sing-song dialect and the old town architecture.

Thessaly

Featuring sprawling meadows dotted with cattle and a bright, verdant landscape more akin to parts of Switzerland than to the picture of Greece most of us harbour, the central region of Greece still relies heavily on agriculture as its main form of industry. I now like to call it 'Middle Greece' on account of its rolling hills, pastures and impressive medieval monasteries that teeter atop dramatic precipices like something out of a fantasy film. As in any rural, farming community, meat makes up a good portion of the diet. I was plied with juicy steaks by my hosts here, though the recipes that have made it into this book are veggie and vegan, using organic eggs from local hens for *strapatsada* (Village Eggs with Tomatoes; see page 144) and the best-quality honey in all the land for *melomakarona* (Honey Biscuits; see pages 208–9).

The Peloponnese

The Peloponnese is a landscape of wild, impenetrable mountains, indigo blue waves thrashing at coastline and in between, olive groves upon olive grove, in which are dotted medieval towers, citadels and pretty villages built of stone. They say locals in the Peloponnese are fierce, but the landscape is fiercer, more rugged in its beauty than perhaps anywhere else in Greece. Olive oil, for obvious reasons, features heavily in the diet here, as do aromatic herbs in dishes like *bakaliaros plaki* (Cod Bake; see page 180) and handmade pasta, which are also staples.

Thessaloniki and northern Greece
Greece's official capital of gastronomy, the city of Thessaloniki is ring-fenced by grand Byzantine city walls, and it is where Greeks go to eat. The reason behind the region's culinary kudos lies in its multi-ethnic past, as the second great city to Constantinople (modern-day Istanbul) in the Ottoman Empire. Before the fall of the empire, Muslims, Jews, Slavs, Italians and Spaniards all lived alongside each other in 'Salonika', exchanging dishes from their corners of the world. Greeks were actually once the minority ethnic group in the city. Pontic Greeks who had previously lived in the mountains of Pontus in Anatolia and were expelled in the great population exchange of 1922 brought their aptitude for rolling filo pastry back to Thessaloniki with them from further east. We have this great culinary clash of cultures to thank for *bourek*, *bougatsa* and *pites* (see pages 96, 38–9, 66–7 and 213) and for flavourful smoked aubergine (eggplant) dishes (see page 68).

The Cyclades
Perhaps the most well-known region of all Greece, the Cyclades is the group of islands home to the white-washed homes and sun-scorched landscapes of Greek summer holidays, but there's much more to see here than the clubs of Mykonos and the caldera of Santorini. Thanks to fertile volcanic ground, some of the nation's best wine is produced in the Cyclades. The same goes for tomatoes. Rugged coastlines here produce enormous capers, which make the traditional village salad far superior to the standard feta, tomato, cucumber and onion combo. Thanks to a wealth of quality ingredients, dishes of the Cyclades are simple in composition and bold in flavour, like a hearty *fourtalia* (Egg and Potato Omelette; see page 100) or spearmint-spiked *tomatokeftedes* (Tomato Fritters; see page 32).

Athens and the Saronic Gulf
From the gritty *stoas* (arcades) of Athens' central market on Athinas Street to the smart, modernist architecture of Kolonaki and on to the leafy suburbs of Kifissia, Athens is a city that has drawn in families with roots from all over the Hellenic world. Becoming the Athens we know today, with its white *polykatoikies* (apartment blocks) in the 1960s, the city's food culture has developed with its population. In this city, you can find *gyros* and Greek coffee on every corner, as well as Georgian bakeries, Kurdish eateries and food from the Levant (see page 48).

Hop across the water to Aegina in the Saronic Gulf and you'll be treated to pistachio ice cream, pistachio bars, pistachio cake – as many pistachios as you can eat, because someone, quite wisely, brought them to the island from Iran in the 1800s and they've flourished there ever since (see page 202–3).

Crete
Greeks speak with reverence when they speak of Crete. Perhaps it's because of the sheer number of times the islanders revolted against the Ottoman Empire, managing to rule themselves as an independent state for a period before becoming a part of the Greek state. Far-flung from the rest of the country in the geographic sense, Crete has developed a unique food culture that depends on the produce of the island itself. In fact, most of the fruit and vegetables eaten in Greece are grown in Crete. *Dakos* (Barley Rusk

Salad; see page 94), *gamopilafo* (Wedding Risotto; see page 158), *kohli bourbouristi* (Sautéed Snails; see page 58) and fiery *raki* (a kind of Cretan grappa) are a source of Cretan pride. Don't try and tell a Cretan you don't like their food, you may not make it back from there alive.

The Dodecanese and Cyprus

Between pine forests and forgotten peaks that jut into the clouds are remote villages on the islands situated furthest away from the Greek mainland. The north of Cyprus has been occupied by Turkey since the 1970s. From Kastellorizo, Rhodes and Mytilene, the shores of Turkey can be seen, even on a cloudy day. Locals pop to the Turkish mainland for their grocery shopping or else eat the same dishes (albeit with slightly different sounding names) to their Turkish neighbours (see pages 186 and 234). The kitchens of the Dodecanese and Cyprus, as well as those cooking within them, hold clues to just how entangled Greek culture is with Turkish. The food here isn't Greek. Neither is it Turkish. Instead, it is a symbol of the power that food has to cross boundaries, borders, religions and beliefs.

*A note in my defence

On reading this section, some may wonder why I've missed certain islands, regions or recipes off the list. The reason is simple – unfortunately, though I wish I could have, I just couldn't make it to every corner of Greece when I was travelling and documenting all the amazing yiayiades I met. I wish I could have gone to even more far-flung destinations, but there's always next time.

HOW I'D LOVE FOR YOU TO USE THIS BOOK

Yiayia is a distillation of my heritage and everything I hold dear about Greece. More than just a cookbook, it holds the ingredients to a way of life that makes me truly happy. There's an emphasis on slowing down to cook, taking time to make a recipe so that the process is a meditative act that can bring just as much joy as the eating. There's a focus, too, on eating with the seasons, as Yiayia does, taking care to nourish ourselves while also being respectful to the land we're privileged to tread.

Along with the recipes of the grandmothers we cooked with, I've included recipes from Greek chefs, producers and friends who work in food along with a dedication (in their words) to their own yiayia. I have been moved to tears by some of these dedications and hope you will find them as emotive and powerful as I have.

MEASUREMENTS, (IM)PRECISION AND INGREDIENTS

Yiayia has a very hard time measuring anything. She doesn't own a pair of kitchen scales or a measuring jug and neither is she happy when I start asking her to count out how many spoons of olive oil she's adding to a certain dish. It transpires that many of Greece's yiayiades are like my own, so I will preface this entire book with an important note that each of them has made abundantly clear to me: season to your own taste and keep sampling as you go along. If a lemon doesn't feel very juicy, have a taste of the dressing and add a squeeze more from a second lemon. If you prefer a bit more of a kick in your spicy pasta, by all means add another teaspoon of cayenne pepper.

Much to my Italian man's horror, I don't like to be too prescriptive with recipes, so I've added options here and there that I've experimented with and have worked for me. I like to add finely sliced fennel and chickpeas (garbanzos) to the Corfiot orange salad (see page 57), for example, just to bulk it up. Generally, Greek yiayiades aren't precious about their recipes. They're far more interested in making something nutritious that tastes really good than they are worried about keeping to strict rules on what should and shouldn't be included in each dish according to tradition.

There are, however, a couple of things that are absolutely non-negotiable:

Olive Oil

It seems outrageous to pour an entire glass of olive oil into a saucepan or baking tray (pan) but that really is what makes these recipes delicious. My jaw drops when I see how many generous glugs of olive oil go into the dishes, especially those we call *ladera* (oily) here in Greece. *Ladera* require plenty of good-quality extra virgin olive oil and there's no getting around it.

Some might think it unhealthy, others wasteful. Greece's matriarchs (I'll include myself in this too) would strongly disagree. It is olive oil that elevates these dishes and makes the simplest of combinations stand out.

Syrup

However much syrup you make will seem like too much but we Greeks were previously Ottoman and the heavily syruped desserts of the east are an inescapable part of our food culture. When testing the *portokalopita* (Orange Pie; see page 238), I was sure the syrup was more than would be needed, but I realised that it was actually just enough and ensured the cake was fresh for days afterwards. In this instance, I think sweet treats aren't supposed to be healthy and tend to live by the belief that a bit of what you fancy does you good.

Seasonality

For as long as I can remember, I have planted and picked tomatoes at home in Corfu with Yiayia. At the age of six, I was ordered to inspect the fruit pre-picking and off I would go, barefoot into the soft fertile clay of our garden to sniff out the juiciest tomatoes for the ever-present village salad at lunch.

Feeling important with the responsibility of choosing the tomatoes that would make up the day's salad, I took my job very seriously. I would lift up the vines, hover, eye-level with each ripe fruit, selecting the plumpest of red baubles and breathing in their verdant summer scent in anticipation of a burst of sweet citric flavour.

Because of this experience, the thought of eating a tomato in winter makes me want to cry. The recipes in this book have been collected, cooked and tested when the produce is in season. In spite of the supermarket's lingering, tempting omnipresence, I hope that you'll be encouraged to seek out local, seasonal produce to make these dishes with too.

USE YOUR HANDS

Experiencing food shouldn't just be about tasting it. 'Ripe and ready' labels on supermarket packaging have really taken the *feeling* of our produce away from us. When Yiayia wants to check if a watermelon is ready to be cut into, she'll knock on it for a hollow sound. She'd be horrified to learn that pre-sliced watermelon exists in plastic packages, no knocking necessary.

There's something almost meditative about feeling your food. The yiayiades in this book often use their hands as whisks or spoons, mixing cake ingredients in large plastic bowls with their fingers splayed out or squishing tomatoes in their palms. I love nothing more than using my hands to roll balls for *keftedes* (meatballs) or taking a time out with the radio on to carefully wrap up *dolmadakia* (stuffed vine leaves) in slick, preserved vine leaves.

The sensations of cooking are almost as important as the sensations of eating. They help us to connect with our food.

TIMINGS

None of the women in this book prescribe to recipes and have laughed at me every time I attempt to weigh out their ingredients. Similarly, they rarely take note of what temperature their oven is on, and prefer to stick a fork in to see if something is done rather than using a timer. I've met their relaxed approach somewhere in the middle, testing the recipes as I go and making a note where you might want to keep an eye on the food. Not all ovens or stoves are made the same, so do as these yiayiades do and get a sense for 'feeling' your food as you go. This also includes taking the time to prepare your meal mindfully and avoiding cutting corners, like letting your butter (lima) beans or chickpeas (garbanzos) soak overnight. It is genuinely better to blitz the onions for a *pastitsada* rather than quickly chopping them, because the *sugo* will be silkier in the end. Grating a tomato or removing the skin might also feel like a hassle, but many of these women swear that it's better on the stomach and sweeter on the tastebuds to do so.

MEAT ON SUNDAYS

I didn't have to try hard to fill the pages of this book with delicious vegetarian and vegan recipes. That's because traditionally, our yiayiades here in Greece eat meat only on Sundays. They also observe 'Sarakosti' (Lent) and commit to *nistia* (fasting), adopting a vegan diet for the period before certain Orthodox holidays. My own yiayia won't touch eggs or dairy on a Wednesday or a Friday throughout the year. Of course, she doesn't do this because of the damage that industrial farming has on the environment, or because she feels particularly strongly about animal rights, but I still admire her commitment to the veggies.

The Feasting chapter in this book is where you'll find the most meat and fish dishes. I hope they impress at your dinner parties or Sunday lunches, as they have done at mine.

sharing

YIAYIA ANASTASIA'S MEDITERRANEAN ROASTED VEGETABLES FROM CORFU

This is a yiayia classic and a take on the traditional dish *tourlou tourlou*. It's so simple to pull together but packs a flavourful punch through the amount of garlic and olive oil Yiayia Anastasia uses. I like to make a huge tray of this so that there's enough left for a salad the next day, which I'll bulk up with quinoa or couscous. It's also a great accompaniment to roast chicken, should you fancy adding a little Greek flavour to your Sunday roast.

Serves 4
Vegan

150 ml (5 fl oz/scant ⅔ cup)
    olive oil
2 red onions, chopped
½ bulb of garlic, cloves crushed
    or finely chopped
20 g (¾ oz) parsley leaves, chopped
2 heaped tablespoons dried
    oregano
1 tablespoon sea salt flakes
1 teaspoon ground black pepper
350 g (12 oz) carrots
300 g (10½ oz) large courgettes
    (zucchini)
400 g (14 oz) aubergines (eggplants)
300 g (10½ oz) green (bell) peppers
400 g (14 oz) potatoes, peeled and
    cut into wedges
2 tomatoes or 2 handfuls of cherry
    tomatoes, sliced or quartered
1 glass of water

TO SERVE
Traditional Tzatziki (see page 25)
feta
sourdough bread

Preheat the oven to 200°C (425°F/gas 7) and line a large roasting tin with baking parchment.

In a bowl, mix together the oil, onions, garlic, parsley, oregano, salt and pepper until combined.

Slice the tops off the carrots, courgettes and aubergines.

Slice lengthways into the peppers, courgettes and aubergines twice (once on each side) but don't halve them – cut into them just enough to make an indentation running the length of the vegetable.

Stuff these indentations with some of the olive oil and herb mixture. Transfer the peppers, courgettes and aubergines to the prepared roasting tin.

Now drop the carrots, potatoes and tomatoes into the bowl with the olive oil mixture and toss to coat.

Arrange these vegetables in the roasting tin around the courgettes, aubergines and peppers.

Add the water to the remaining olive oil mixture and then pour what is remaining into the roasting tin.

Add an extra crack of black pepper, then transfer to the oven and roast for 1–1½ hours. During that time, if you see that the vegetables are taking on a little too much colour, turn them over or cover with foil to prevent them from burning. Yiayia Anastasia likes to cook this for as long as possible so that the flavours develop.

Serve with a blob of tzatziki, a chunk of feta and a good wedge of sourdough.

YIAYIA ANASTASIA'S TRADITIONAL TZATZIKI FROM CORFU

Serves 4–6
Vegetarian

300 g (10½ oz) good-quality Greek
  yoghurt (it must be creamy and
  dense, such as Fage)
100 g (3½ oz) cucumber
4 garlic cloves (or 2 large cloves),
  crushed or very finely chopped
squeeze of lemon juice
handful of dill, finely chopped
1 black kalamata olive
sea salt and freshly ground
  black pepper

Put the yoghurt in a bowl.

On a surface covered with a kitchen towel you don't mind getting
a little messy, grate the cucumber (skin and all), then strain out any
excess water using the towel to wring out the moisture from the
cucumber (best to do this over a bowl or sink).

Add the drained cucumber to the bowl with the yoghurt, then add
most of the garlic.

Mix well, then add lemon juice to taste and a pinch of salt and
pepper. Taste and adjust the seasoning, adding more garlic if you
can handle the kick.

Transfer to a serving bowl and sprinkle over the dill.

Top the tzatziki with the single olive, to serve in the traditional
Greek taverna style.

YIAYIA ANASTASIA

Born Corfu, 1937

'When I first married and I had my two children, we were so poor that we slept on the floor. In those years it was still difficult here, no one had any money and tourism wasn't a thing. We had two rooms in the house and that was it. It wasn't just us living in this house either. I moved in with my in-laws. They slept in one room and my husband Giorgi, the children and I all slept in the adjoining room. We couldn't afford beds, so we slept on hay-filled mattresses.

Before I moved in, the house was just a small shack with animals running in and out – cows lived here. It wasn't until I came to Perivoli village from the next village along that they moved the animals out and built a proper house with plumbing and electricity.

We would eat vegetables because that was what we could grow and what the odd neighbour would have to give us. We still exchange fruit and vegetables here in the village. If I grow too many peppers, I'll give some to my sister Stamatella and she'll give me the wild greens she picks. Life hasn't changed for us much and we don't ask for a lot – just enough rain for a good harvest.'

THEIA STAMATELLA'S TSIGARELLI (SPICY WILD GREENS) FROM CORFU

Theia (aunt) Stamatella is my yiayia's younger sister, and is famous in our family for her *tsigarelli*. Like her signature dish of wild greens with plenty of spice, Stamatella is warming and strong in equal measure. She's lived difficult moments and raised her children alone in a Greek village at a time when single motherhood in rural Greece was unheard of and most definitely frowned upon. Like everything in life though, she did it with grace and kindness.

She is the aunt whose face fills with joy and eyes stream with happy tears when she sees me. She's the one my British mother and I have fled to for comfort after too many harsh words from Yiayia. She will travel across the country at a moment's notice to offer extra care for her grandchildren's new-born babies. A Corfiot fairy godmother.

I've tweaked her *tsigarelli* recipe slightly in regards to the *horta* (wild greens) Stamatella uses, because the *horta* she forages in Corfu can be impossible to find, even in the rest of Greece. This dish is a great way to use up old beetroot, carrot and fennel tops, it's super simple to make and is best served with crusty bread to soak up all that oil. I've actually also tried this as a sauce for pasta, which yielded great results.

Make sure to use a combination of greens and be aware that if you're using spinach, it will wilt more than other greens, so it's best to add it to the pan when there is just 5 minutes of cooking time left. Always include the stems of the greens – you want all the goodness in there.

Serves 4
Vegan

800 g (1 lb 12 oz) wild greens with their stems (can be a selection of beetroot/beet, carrot and fennel tops as well as chervil, nettles, spinach and dandelion), washed thoroughly
400 ml (13 fl oz/generous 1½ cups) water
150 ml (5 fl oz/scant ⅔ cup) olive oil
1 tablespoon ground black pepper
1 tablespoon paprika
1 teaspoon ground cinnamon
1 hot red chilli
5 cloves
½ tablespoon salt
125 g (4 oz) tinned tomatoes or fresh tomato, grated

Put all the ingredients into a large saucepan, bring to the boil and then simmer over a medium heat for 20–30 minutes until most of the water has evaporated and the sauce has come together nicely.

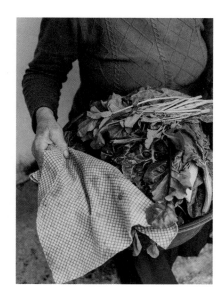

THEIA STAMATELLA

Born Corfu, 1940

'I built my kitchen outhouse with its wood-fired oven myself when I was eight months pregnant. I would say it's been a tough life. Years ago, our mothers just gave birth to babies one after the other. I was one of ten children, and it was my elder siblings who were left to take care of me, some of whom stole my food.

It was the years of the war and post-war and we didn't have much to eat on the island. We had to make do with what we had. This is why women my age all know which wild greens to pick to put into a *tsigarelli*. There are all sorts of wild greens we can make it with.

It didn't get better when I got married. My husband left me when I was 33 years old, still young and in my prime. He just decided to go and start a new life in America. We had three children together at the time. My eldest was only eight years old. He went to America for 44 years and now he's back and wants to live together like man and wife.

He found a new woman in America and had a child with her. He even sent the boy here a few weeks at a time to learn Greek. He was six years old when he came for the first time, but what could I do? My husband sent him on his own on the plane and I couldn't turn him away. It wasn't his fault.

We never divorced and then five years ago, he showed up and wanted to come and live back in the family home. I didn't want him but my children wanted to give him a chance, so he lives here now but we sleep in separate rooms. Other women in the village have the audacity to ask me why I don't cook for him!

I stayed single for my children, even though I was incredibly young when he left. I didn't go on and meet someone else. Other men wanted me right the way up until my seventies. Of course by that point it was an old man who asked after me, but still. I had a sewing machine and I made money for my family myself. I made it work.'

YIAYIA EVANGELIA'S TOMATOKEFTEDES (TOMATO FRITTERS) FROM SANTORINI

I'm cooking with Yiayia Evangelia off-season in Santorini and it is a different island to the one I've visited in the past. Come summer, the caldera of this ancient volcano will be packed with photo-snapping tourists who cram into the village of Oia to get a glance at the dramatic sloping landscape and its now-famous white cube homes. Before the tourists, though, there were people like Eva, who have known and lived this island in very different circumstances.

She makes me cry with the poems she has written for loved ones and tells me stories of transcendent experiences she's had in life. Spiritual and devoutly religious, she still mourns the loss of her husband, Carlos, and when she speaks about him, I have a strong sense of her loss.

Together we make *tomatokeftedes* using Santorini's top produce: the tomato. The volcanic soil makes Santorini the perfect tomato-growing spot. Each and every one of the tomatoes I sneak into my mouth is a juicy, sweet burst of delight. When you're shopping for produce for this dish, ensure you sample the tomatoes and choose ones in season, with plenty of flavour.

Serves 4–6
Vegan

500 g (1 lb 2 oz) cherry tomatoes off the vine
3 red onions, roughly chopped
100 g/3½ oz of spearmint (about 2 large bunches), leaves finely chopped
2 teaspoons dried basil
2 teaspoons fine table salt
1 teaspoon cracked black pepper
300 ml (10 fl oz/1¼ cups) water
500 g (1 lb 2 oz/4 cups) plain (all-purpose) flour
300 ml (10 fl oz/1¼ cups) sunflower oil
Greek yoghurt mixed with chopped dill, to serve

Put the tomatoes into a large bowl, roll up your sleeves and crush them in the bowl by hand. You want to see the juice pop from inside the tomatoes.

Add the red onions and mix in by hand, followed by the chopped spearmint leaves. Mix in the basil, salt and pepper by hand.

Once everything is combined, pour in the water, followed by the flour. Mix by hand until the flour becomes wet and combines with the tomato mixture.

Heat the sunflower oil in a dry, non-stick, deep frying pan (skillet) over a high heat for 1 minute or so until you can drop a tiny amount of your mix into the oil and it begins to rapidly sizzle.

Drop a level tablespoon of the tomato mixture into the hot oil. It doesn't need to be a perfect shape – yiayiades care about flavour. Cook three or four tomatokeftedes at a time, depending on how many tablespoons of mixture can fit into your pan. You want space between each one so that they don't stick together and become a clump. Fry for 2–3 minutes on one side, then use a spoon to lift from the underside and turn the *tomatokeftedes* over and fry for a further 1–2 minutes until they are crisp and reddish-brown all over. The frying time will become faster as the oil heats up, so check the undersides to ensure they aren't burning.

Remove the *tomatokeftedes* with a slotted spoon and drain on paper towels. Serve with Greek yoghurt and dill for dipping.

YIAYIA EVANGELIA

Born Santorini, 1958

'The dishes I make are at least four generations old, and here on the island we cook with what is available to us. We're well known for our tomatoes, so many of our most traditional dishes include them.

I fast before special saint days as well as Easter and Christmas, so dishes like this are an important part of my diet. We Orthodox Christians don't eat meat or dairy when we fast, and some don't even allow themselves olive oil. I think it's important to have these periods of self-restraint; it doesn't just do good to the body, it purifies your mind. I find there's more clarity and reflection when I fast. It's a spiritual experience to cleanse.

Life on the island has changed so much in my lifetime. When I was a little girl, to get anywhere we would go by donkey, not by car. Before there were roads and tourists we were an island of fields and fields of fava (yellow split peas), tomatoes and grapevines.'

YIAYIA KATINA'S PRASSOPITA
(LEEK PIE) FROM FLORINA

Born Meliti, Florina, 1939

Dedication by Meni Valle, food educator and cookbook author

Florina in northern Greece is where my family is from. Along with its beautiful mountain landscape and stunning lakes, this region is famous for its *pites* (pies). This is one of my favourites.

My mother, Katina, migrated to Australia in the late 1950s, as many did in those days, in search of a better life. For my mother it was a little more than that. She followed her heart and travelled to Australia to be with my father, Kosta, her fiancé at the time.

I never met my own grandmothers, but I'm forever grateful that my children had my mother as their yiayia. I still remember their little faces when they were young, covered in icing (confectioner's) sugar when my mother would allow them to have *kourabiedes* (almond biscuits/cookies) with a glass of milk for breakfast. I loved the way she would prepare whatever meal they asked for; nothing was ever too much trouble.

My mother's kitchen was always inviting and filled with warmth, her favourite Greek tunes usually playing in the background. I adored being among the chatter and laughter, my mother in charge and instructing my father and myself of jobs to be done.

She would have bowls of fillings for a *pita* arranged on the kitchen bench. Balls of dough sitting on a tablecloth resting at the kitchen table, waiting patiently to be rolled out into paper-thin sheets, ready to assemble the *pita*.

Serves 4–6
Vegetarian

FOR THE RUSTIC FILO PASTRY
500 g (1 lb 2 oz/4 cups) strong white
   bread flour, plus extra for dusting
2 teaspoons salt
2 tablespoons olive oil
1 tablespoon apple cider vinegar
250 ml (8½ fl oz/1 cup) warm water

FOR THE FILLING
1 kg (2 lb 4 oz) leeks, finely sliced
plenty of olive oil, for frying and
   brushing
300 g (10½ oz) feta, crumbled
3 eggs
60 ml (2 fl oz/¼ cup) whole milk
salt and freshly ground black
   pepper

First make the pastry. Sift the flour and salt into a large bowl.
Make a well in the centre and pour in the olive oil, vinegar and
warm water. Mix the flour into the liquid mixture slowly until it
comes together. Add a little more water if you need to.

Knead the mixture into a soft and elastic dough, then form it into
a ball, cover the bowl with a cloth and leave to rest for 1 hour. While
the dough is resting, prepare your filling.

Sauté the leeks with a little oil in a frying pan (skillet) until softened,
about 1 minute.

Once soft, remove from the heat and transfer to a large bowl,
then add the feta, egg and milk and season to taste. Mix well, then
set aside.

Preheat the oven to 180°C (400°F/gas 6).

Divide the dough into four balls. On a lightly floured surface, roll
one of the balls out into a sheet using a long, thin rolling pin. Keep
rolling in all directions until you have a large, round and very fine
sheet that is so thin that you can see your hand through it. Repeat
with the remaining balls.

Prepare a 23 x 33 cm (9 x 13 inch) baking dish (*tapsi*) by brushing
with olive oil. You can now place a sheet of filo in the dish – it
should be about 5 cm (2 inches) larger than the baking dish, so you
have enough pastry to fold over once finished to make a crimped
edge. Brush the pastry with oil, then top with another sheet.

Top the two sheets with the filling and cover with the remaining
two filo sheets, again brushing with olive oil between the sheets. The
edges of the pastry should fall out over the dish. Fold these back in
on themselves, then gently crimp them so they create a 'rim', which
will form a nice crust when baked.

Score the pastry into portions and brush generously with olive oil,
including the edges. Sprinkle with a little water before baking in the
oven for 30–40 minutes until crisp and golden.

YIAYIA THEODORA'S HORTOPITA (WILD GREENS AND FETA PIE) FROM PONTUS

Yiayia Theodora is a filo-rolling queen. She moves so fast that I can't keep up with her, flicking her long, thin *verga* (a special rolling pin for pastry) back and forth across her Formica table to create ultra-fine sheets of pastry for our *hortopita*.

I'm in the far north of Greece, in Theodora's village of Asprovalta. I've driven past misty fields, thick in a blanket of fog, making the journey from Thessaloniki seem almost mystical. This is a world away from the light, bright Greece I know. Giant pines line the road and the countryside stretches on for miles. There's a definite sense of being near the Balkans here – the weather more treacherous, the landscape wilder.

Yiayia Theodora is a proud 'Pontia'. For generations, the Pontic Greeks lived in Pontus, on the Black Sea and in north-eastern Anatolia. Yiayia Theodora's family, along with many others, migrated from there to northern Greece, bringing their indecipherable dialect and incredible *pita*-crafting culture with them. While *spanakopita* has made it into the mainstream, *hortopita* like the one Theodora makes is a rarer find. What makes this one so special is the combination of greens and herbs for a wholesome, flavourful filling.

Pack it in your picnic to share or else snack on this for days. On first sight it may look like a lot of greens, but they wilt down a lot in the pan, so don't skimp on the good stuff. You can easily make this a vegan recipe by omitting the eggs and feta.

Serves 6–8
Vegetarian

1 kg (2 lb 4 oz) spinach
1 kg (2 lb 4 oz) wild or mixed greens (can be a combination of beetroot/beet and carrot tops, chervil, rocket/arugula, wild chicory, dandelion and nettles), washed thoroughly
bunch of parsley
handful of peppermint leaves
3 tablespoons salt
olive oil, for frying
8 spring onions (scallions), finely chopped
3 large eggs, beaten
300 g (10½ oz) feta, crumbled
1 x recipe quantity Rustic Filo Pastry (see page 39)

Put the greens and herbs into a large bowl. Add 2 tablespoons of the salt, toss and set aside for 5 minutes.

Heat a splash of oil in a large non-stick frying pan (skillet) or wok over a medium heat, then add the spring onions and sweat for 1–2 minutes.

Meanwhile, fill the bowl of greens with water, then tip out into a colander, squeezing the leaves with your hands to remove any extra moisture – this will help to avoid a soggy *pita*. Add the drained greens to the frying pan with the spring onions, stirring and folding the leaves in with a wooden spoon. Continue like this for up to 5 minutes while the water from the leaves evaporates, then transfer back to the colander to strain one last time before setting aside and allowing to cool.

When the greens are cool, add the eggs and feta and mix well. Your Pontic hortopita filling is ready to go. Roll out the pastry dough, fill the pie and bake as per the instructions on page 39.

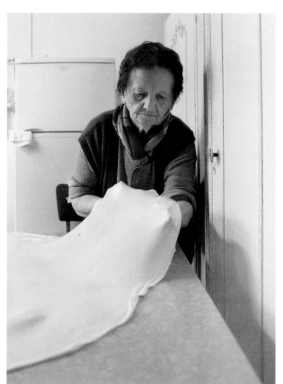

YIAYIA THEODORA

Born Drama, 1934

'These *pites* and the way we make them originated with the Pontics in Turkey. Lots of Greeks were refugees in our own country, once upon a time. My family had to leave Cappadocia, but we have managed to keep our language, Pontic Greek. We're still proud of our roots and so we're one of the few ethnic groups that has held onto its dialect here in Greece. If I speak it now, you won't be able to understand me. It's something between Turkish, Greek and Slavic.

My own father was killed by Bulgarians when I was only seven years old. The Bulgarians were trying to take territory in my village and they rounded up all the men, took them to the schoolyard and shot them. I heard gun fire and didn't know it was my father that was being killed until afterwards. I heard it all from the village. Then I found out it was my father that had been shot and without a moment's notice we had to leave with nothing. It was the dead of winter and so cold it was snowing, and we had to walk without proper coats through the snow to get to Thessaloniki from Drama. I don't wish that kind of hardship on anyone.

Thankfully, God gave me my husband when I was just 17 and we've been inseparable ever since. I've only ever been with one man in my life. I swear to you, I was intact for him like the day I was born. We didn't have this rubbing up with one man, rubbing up with another, type thing. What are these things that young people do these days? Only with my husband!'

YIAYIA FEYROUZ'S LEVANTINE TABBOULEH
FROM TOKAÇLI (TURKEY)

On a bright weekday afternoon in Athens, I manage to grab Feyrouz at her eponymous downtown eatery to ask if she might be up for cooking together for the book. She emerges into the sun-drenched street, where I'm eating one of her famous Levantine *lahmacuns*, beaming a greeting at me and hugging me despite never having met me before. 'This is my kind of woman,' I think.

In a few years, Feyrouz (the downtown establishment) has become an Athenian institution, offering an alternative to the ubiquitous souvlaki and bringing Levantine cuisine and its rich history to the city. Every lunchtime there's a line of customers that snakes out of the door and spills into the street, but she never seems phased by this and always has time to chat to her regulars.

Together we make a mighty duo of tabbouleh (like no other I've ever had in my life, perhaps owing to the incredible combination of spices) and beetroot (beet) hummus (better and prettier than your regular kind) . I like the idea of these always being eaten together, but of course, you can make them separately.

Serves 6
Vegan

250 g (9 oz/generous 1⅓ cups) bulgur wheat
1 heaped tablespoon red pepper paste
1 teaspoon ground cumin (Feyrouz uses wild mountain cumin)
2 teaspoons dried peppermint
2 teaspoons table salt
150 g (5 oz) parsley (about 2 bunches), leaves finely chopped
10–15 leaves seasonal salad greens, such as lettuce or cabbage, finely chopped, plus extra leaves to serve
100 g (3½ oz) tomatoes, peeled and finely chopped
200 g (7 oz) spring onions (scallions), whites finely chopped
50 g (2 oz) spearmint leaves, finely chopped
1 large carrot, grated
50 ml (1¾ fl oz/3 tablespoons) pomegranate molasses
juice of 1 lemon
110 ml (3¾ fl oz/scant ½ cup) olive oil

First prepare the bulgur wheat. Put the bulgur wheat in a large bowl, cover with boiling water and leave for 3 minutes, then strain the water out and leave the bulgur wheat to cool.

Once cool, add the red pepper paste, ground cumin, peppermint and salt. Next, add the parsley, salad greens, tomatoes, spring onions, spearmint and carrot and gently mix together.

Finally, mix together the pomegranate molasses, lemon juice and olive oil in a jug (pitcher) or jar and pour over the tabbouleh. Stir well and serve immediately. If you want to eat the tabbouleh later, reserve the dressing and mix it in just before serving.

Serves the tabbouleh Levantine village style, with crunchy lettuce leaves to scoop up huge mouthfuls of tabbouleh.

YIAYIA FEYROUZ'S LEVANTINE BEETROOT HUMMUS FROM TOKAÇLI (TURKEY)

Serves 4
Vegan

325 g (11½ oz) beetroot (beets)
75 g (2½ oz) celeriac (celery root),
  peeled and roughly chopped
50 g (2 oz) tahini
1 teaspoon salt
2 small garlic cloves or 1 large
  garlic clove, chopped
2 tablespoons room-temperature
  water
juice of 1 lemon
1 teaspoon ground cumin (Feyrouz
  uses wild mountain cumin)
handful of sunflower and pumpkin
  seeds
olive oil, to serve

Preheat the oven to 150°C (325°F/gas 3).

Bring a saucepan of water to the boil and boil the beetroot for 25–30 minutes until you can stick a fork through it, then allow to cool before peeling its skin off. Keep the beetroot water.

Chop the peeled beetroot into quarters and add to a large bowl along with the other ingredients, except the seeds.

Mix the ingredients by hand or with a wooden spoon at first, ensuring everything is incorporated, then transfer the mixture to a food processor and blitz. You may need to do this in batches, depending on the size of your food processor. Don't blend too much – Feyrouz likes her beetroot hummus chunky.

Spread the seeds out on a baking sheet and roast in the oven for 5–7 minutes, then remove and allow to cool slightly.

Serve the hummus dressed with a drizzle of olive oil and a sprinkling of the toasted seeds.

YIAYIA FEYROUZ

Born Antioch, 1961

'Tokaçlı, where I am from, is about half an hour from Aleppo and is considered the Levant. The Levant itself as a geographical area comprised modern-day Lebanon, Syria, Turkey, Palestine and Israel. The cuisine is so diverse because the Silk Road passed through the Levant, and it took influence from Persian dishes, too. People have no idea how majestic the Persian kitchen or the cuisine from Baghdad was – that combination of sour and sweet in the foods. It dates back to the 9th century and has an incredible history.

My home was a beautiful place – a paradise, with so many olive trees. My family was in the minority of Orthodox Christians in the area and we went by the term 'Rumi'. It referred to the pre-Islamic Christian minorities that had resided in Antioch (modern-day Antakya) since the days of Byzantium. By the time I was engaged, at 19, and came to Athens, I wanted to leave because I didn't have a life there as a young woman. It wasn't safe for me to go out because I was part of a religious minority. There's absolutely no way I could get on a bus there and wear my cross around my neck. Even the boys had problems and had to change their surnames to sound more Turkish. It wasn't even legal for us to speak Greek at the time. I learned Turkish at school and then Arabic out of school and the Greek we spoke was only between us family members or a lady called Despina who taught me how to cook.

It was a need to start Feyrouz, not a want. I had retired from my job at a gold jeweller's and I wanted to cook. I had some experience cooking privately at people's houses, but I had a real need to open my own place. Sometimes I used to think "Oh God, what have I done?" when I saw the line outside the door, but then I'd become enthusiastic about how many people wanted to eat my food and come running down the stairs to the kitchen to make more.'

YIAYIA ARGYRO'S BAKED GAVROS (ANCHOVIES) FROM VOLOS

Yiayia Argyro lives in Volos, a port town by the sea famed for its seafood meze, the biting alcoholic drink, *tsipouro*, and Jason (of Jason and the Argonauts). On any given night of the week, Volos' *tsipouradika* are full of people. At these decades-old establishments, priority is given to the drink itself, with a small of plate of seafood served for every order of *tsipouro*. The more *tsipouro* you order, the fancier each plate of meze becomes.

You'd think this system might yield catastrophic results, but the *tsipouro* actually serves as a digestif, which means you can squeeze in a little more food. Always good news to me.

It seems only right, then, that I sample a classic meze plate with Argyro. In really no time at all she rustles up a tray of gavros and serves it with a glass of *tsipouro* and crusty bread out in the sunshine. Greek summer on a plate.

Serves 4

800 g (1 lb 12 oz) fresh anchovies, gutted, heads removed and rinsed under running water
1 tablespoon sea salt flakes
1 teaspoon ground black pepper
2 tablespoons dried oregano
1 red (bell) pepper, chopped
3 garlic cloves
1 lemon, sliced
extra virgin olive oil, for cooking

Preheat the oven to 200°C (425°F/gas 7).

Place the anchovies in a baking tray (pan), then sprinkle with the salt, pepper and oregano.

Sprinkle over the red pepper, followed by the whole peeled garlic cloves and slices of lemon. Finally, drizzle with a good glug of olive oil and bake in the oven for 20–25 minutes until lightly browned.

YIAYIA ARGYRO

Born Evoia, 1938

'Volos has changed a lot since I was a young girl, but the *tsipouro* has always been an important part of our culture here. All the men have their *steki* (hangout) and it's only to that spot that they will go for a *tsipouro*. It used to be a thing my generation did early, before lunchtime. The fishermen would finish their own shift around 10 a.m. and then they'd fill up the *tsipouradika* for a meze and a drink before going home to their wives for lunch.'

YIAYIA VASILIKI'S ZORKA PIE
FROM CORFU

Vasiliki is a young yiayia. Not originally from Corfu, but with an encyclopedic knowledge of Corfiot cooking, she runs the Ambelonas farmhouse restaurant set in verdant countryside just outside of the island's Venetian old town. The building itself has been there since the 1600s and Vasiliki's family history can be traced back to the Venetian settlers on the island.

Inspired by her mother-in-law's handwritten recipe book – filled with forgotten island recipes that even my own yiayia has never heard of – Vasiliki set about learning all there is to know about traditional Corfiot cuisine and applying it (with a few tweaks of her own) to her restaurant's menu.

This zorka pie (meaning 'naked', on account of it not requiring any pastry) is just one of the lost Corfiot village dishes that I'd never heard of before meeting Vasiliki. It's light, verging on a quiche, is packed full of greens and, in true Corfiot style, has a spicy kick.

Serves 4–6
Vegetarian

2 tablespoons extra virgin olive oil, plus extra for greasing
2 red onions, roughly chopped
2 large garlic cloves, finely sliced
800 g (1 lb 12 oz) courgettes (zucchini), grated
60 g (2 oz) chopped fresh herbs, stalks included (Vasiliki uses a mix of dill, parsley, thyme, marjoram and spearmint)
2 spring onions (scallions), chopped (use the whole onion; swap for leeks if not in season)
200 g (7 oz) good-quality Greek yoghurt
120 ml (4 fl oz/½ cup) milk
2 eggs
pinch each of dried basil, dried marjoram, dried oregano, dried mint, sweet paprika, cayenne pepper and ground cloves
1 teaspoon ground coriander
½ teaspoon ground black pepper
250 g (9 oz) feta, crumbled
3–5 tablespoons rolled oats, plus extra for the dish
grated Parmesan, graviera or pecorino, to finish
sea salt

Preheat the oven to 160°C (350°F/gas 4).

Heat the olive oil in a large frying pan (skillet) over a low heat and fry the onions for 2 minutes, then add the garlic and cook until they are soft and caramelised, about another 2 minutes. Remove from the heat and allow to cool.

In a bowl, combine the courgettes with the herbs, spring onions, yoghurt, milk and eggs, then add the herbs and spices. Fold the feta and onions and garlic into the mixture and stir to combine. Depending on the saltiness of your feta, you can also add a pinch of sea salt at this stage.

Finally, add the oats to soak up some of the liquid from the vegetables. The amount you will need will depend on how wet your mixture is.

Generously grease the bottom of a ceramic or Pyrex baking dish with olive oil and sprinkle in some more oats to cover the base of the dish with a fine layer. Pour in your zorka mix, followed by a generous sprinkle of grated cheese.

Bake for 40–45 minutes until the top of the pie is golden.

YIAYIA VASILIKI

Born Sparta, 1956

'This is a typical village pie. People use whatever they have available for it, so I like to keep my recipe loose with this. The whole idea is to put a good quantity of herbs in there, but you can choose each one according to your taste. I don't like to be a slave to a recipe. If you don't have courgette (zucchini) or it's not in season, you can use pumpkin or carrot instead. This recipe should just be a guideline for the dish.

It's not essential to the recipe, but marjoram is used a lot here in Corfu. We use it in many dishes but there's a difference between village cooking and *hora* (town) cooking. The dishes from Corfu town were more elaborate and time consuming and were often made by kitchen staff for their rich, Venetian employers. Village dishes like this are much easier to prepare.

There's a tradition on the island to prepare spice mixes for certain dishes. Obviously if you don't have the mix for this one ready, you can just add a pinch of each spice. Many families like ours have a mix ready to go for each dish. We have a thing for spices here in Corfu, thanks to the Venetians and their involvement in the spice trade. We have a lot to thank the Italians for.'

YIAYIA VASILIKI'S NERATZOSALATA
(SPICY ORANGE SALAD) FROM CORFU

Owing to a very humid climate and cataclysmic winters here in Corfu, the island is blessed with fruit trees that bear treasure. In the cooler months and well into spring, Corfu's citrus trees flourish, and we struggle to use the many kumquats, lemons and oranges that hang heavy on our branches. This orange salad is just one of the ways we incorporate our swag of hefty orange baubles into our diets.

Refreshing and juicy but with a punchy kick, this *neratzosalata* is one I love to serve as an accompaniment to meat. It's especially nice with a roast chicken on a Sunday and it's so simple to throw together.

Yiayia Vasiliki uses just four ingredients when we make this classic Corfiot dish together, but I sometimes like to bulk it up with finely sliced fennel, baked chickpeas (garbanzos) and fennel fronds. In that sense, it can become a standalone dish. A good-quality olive oil makes all the difference here.

Serves 4
Vegan

2–3 juicy oranges, peeled then sliced into 1 cm (½ inch) thick rounds
good glug of extra virgin olive oil
1 teaspoon spicy paprika or cayenne pepper
pinch of sea salt flakes

Arrange the sliced oranges on a platter or wide plate.

Extravagantly glug the olive oil over the arrangement, then sprinkle over the paprika or cayenne pepper, followed by the sea salt.

YIAYIA EURIDIKI'S KOHLI BOURBOURISTI (SAUTÉED SNAILS) FROM CRETE

Not to everyone's taste, but a delicacy in Crete all the same, Yiayia Euridiki's snails seem to be aware that they're in for it. When released from their fine tulle encasement and popped into a bowl, they try to escape all over Euridiki's retro-tiled kitchen. I can't say I'm not alarmed and I'm having an incredibly hard time playing it cool.

This dish has been eaten in Crete since the ancients roamed these parts. Perhaps even the minotaur might have had a taste for them. More recently, Yiayia Euridiki tells me it was a cheap dish to throw together post-war, when most Cretan families lived in poverty. Snails were free and everyone could get their hands on a sprig or two of rosemary and a splash of vinegar. Now the Cretans even hold a snail festival every year, such is the dish's popularity.

Traditionally, Cretans eat this dish before Orthodox Easter, picking the cooked snails from their shells with a toothpick and swilling them down with *raki*, a kind of Cretan grappa that sets fire to your throat. I like to serve them with rosemary-sprinkled fries or a plate of boiled greens.

A note on prep – it's best to leave your snails without food for up to a week, to ensure whatever they ate before being harvested is well out of their digestive tract, as it sometimes doesn't agree with us humans. Alternatively, feed your snails lettuce, apples or grapevine leaves for a few days before cooking.

Serves 4

500 g (1 lb 2 oz) live snails in their
  shells, washed
1 tablespoon sea salt flakes
good glug of extra virgin olive oil
40 ml (1⅓ fl oz/generous
  2 tablespoons) red wine vinegar
3 sprigs rosemary

Sprinkle the salt into a large, wide frying pan (skillet) over a high heat.

Arrange the live snails, shells up, into the pan so that the snail's body itself is making contact with the pan. Fry for 4 minutes, then add a good glug of olive oil to the pan. Fry for a further 5–6 minutes until the snails have stopped bubbling. Remove from the heat, splash in the red wine vinegar, throw in the rosemary sprigs and eat straight away.

YIAYIA EURIDIKI

Born Crete, 1938

'When we were young, we would run off out into the neighbourhood on a snail hunt whenever it rained. We'd wait and wait for the rains to come, then our parents would send us off to search under rocks once a downpour was over. It was a game for us. I didn't think about it much then, but it was a dish that they could sustain us on with no money at all. The "bourbour" in the name of the dish means to be face down, in our dialect.

Even as we get older, it's the simple things that fill our lives. I'm without my husband now but I still leave the house to see my friends, to eat a dessert, to go swimming in the summer sun. I'm content in the fact that I can still cook, clean my house and wash my dishes. What else could I need?

I'm ready for death, but I'd like it to take me suddenly, at this stage in life while I'm still autonomous. I want my family to find me in my bed. The family tomb's ready and I've made peace with that. Life is good, as long as you can live it.'

KYRIA KATERINA'S LADENIA
(SUMMER FOCACCIA) FROM KIMOLOS

Kyria Katerina is a complete chance encounter. While I'm in Milos to cook with Yiayia Anthousa and Yiayia Antonia, I meet her hanging out her washing. I'm in the holiday rental next to her house, which is right on the water with a view of neighbouring Kimolos island. Traditional fishing *kaikia* boats bob along the turquoise sea that extends from Katerina's home and neighbours constantly pop by to say good morning while we chat.

Within minutes, she's inviting me over to make a *ladenia*, and we stand in the dappled shade of a lemon tree on her sea-view terrace to make what I like to call 'the Greek deep pan'. Originating in Kimolos, just across the water, the *ladenia* is something of a cross between a focaccia and a pizza. Incredibly simple to make and the ultimate picnic snack, it's what the kids of Milos and Kimolos take to the beach with them (the beaches in Milos are some of Greece's best). Sustenance for a long summer day.

Katerina insists that toppings should be restricted to fresh tomatoes, red onions, capers and oregano. I wonder out loud at red peppers and cheese and she cuts me off with a sharp, 'Well, then you're just making a pizza – not *ladenia*.'

Serves 6, or more if part of a meze
Vegan

500 g (1 lb 2 oz/4 cups) plain (all-purpose) flour
1 heaped teaspoon sugar
8 g (1 tablespoon) active dry yeast
230 ml (8 fl oz/scant 1 cup) water
2 teaspoons salt, plus extra to season
2 tablespoons apple cider vinegar
3 tablespoons olive oil, plus extra for drizzling
500 g (1 lb 2 oz) tomatoes (use cherry tomatoes for extra flavour!)
1 large red onion, finely sliced
1 teaspoon dried oregano
1 tablespoon capers

First make the dough. Put the flour into a large bowl and make a well in the middle. To that well, add the sugar, yeast and a splash of the water.

Taking care not to tip it into the well as it will stop your yeast from reacting, add 1 teaspoon of the salt around the edges of the flour, followed by the vinegar and olive oil.

Add the rest of the water, a little at a time, mixing the flour mixture with one hand so that it combines to make a ball of dough.

Knead for up to 10 minutes until the dough stops sticking to the bowl. Add a little extra flour if it continues to stubbornly stick.

After kneading, cover the bowl with a kitchen towel and leave to rise in a warm place for 2 hours, or until the dough has doubled in size.

Preheat the oven to 200°C (425°F/gas 7).

If you're using large tomatoes, take the skins off and cut them into thin slices. If you opt for cherry tomatoes, you don't need to remove the skins, simply slice them.

Put the sliced onion into a bowl, sprinkle it with the remaining salt, then using your hand, gently crush it in your fist. Rinse in a colander.

Prepare a deep 33 x 24 cm (13 x 9½ inch) baking tray (pan) by drizzling it with olive oil until the base is completely covered by a very thin film of oil. Baste the sides of the tray with oil, too, so that your *ladenia* doesn't stick.

Once your dough has doubled in size, spread it across the base of the tray and use your fingertips to pull at its edges and stretch it out so that it reaches all four corners, then make little indentations across the dough with your fingertips.

Layer the sliced tomatoes across the dough, followed by the onions. (When you have good tomatoes, you don't need additional tomato purée (paste), but if your tomatoes are a bit anaemic (as Katerina says), add a little tomato purée mixed with olive oil first, then layer your sliced tomatoes on top.)

Next, add an extra sprinkling of salt (trust me – it really helps with the flavour, especially if you're eating tomatoes out of season!). Finally, top with the oregano, capers and one last, glorious drizzle of olive oil.

Bake in the oven for 35–45 minutes. Check on it halfway through the cooking time to make sure it isn't getting too brown. You want the dough around the sides to be golden and for the onions and capers to also be nicely browned.

KYRIA KATERINA

Born Epirus, 1954

'My husband loved this place so much that when I'm back here from Athens, I feel that sometimes he's still here with me. We met in Athens and I still live there in the winters. I come to Milos for Easter and stay until October. It's a retreat for me. My peace and quiet. Of course, it's terrifying when there's a storm because I'm metres away from the water and all on my own now, but then I wake up on a day like this and I realise how lucky I am.

I'm the host among all my friends because of the house being right on the water. We've had crazy summers here – everyone over, drinking *tsipouro*, dipping in the sea, getting out again for another bite to eat or a drink, staying way past sundown.

This *ladenia* always features as a summer snack. They say the recipe originally comes from Kimolos but I really see Milos and Kimolos as one. They come to us for panigiria festivals (local saints' days) and parties and we go to them. So, the *ladenia* probably hopped over the water at a panigiri at some point or another.

I love my day trips to Kimolos. It's not touristic at all. When I go to a *kafeneion* for my morning coffee with a friend, I can barely have a conversation for the amount of locals that stop by to say *kalimera* (good morning). Whoever walks by, they have a *kalimera* for you. It's lovely.'

YIAYIA MARTHA'S HALLOUMOPITES (HALLOUMI BUNS) FROM CYPRUS

Born Cyprus, 1940

Dedication by Georgina Hayden, award-winning food writer and television presenter

I don't think I can ever recall a time where there haven't been some sort of *pites* in my yiayia's kitchen. She is forever making little breads laced with something or other – usually halloumi or black olives. The latter would also have chopped onions, coriander (cilantro) and be slightly punchier in flavour. The halloumi versions would be more subtle, with just dried mint to flavour the dough – something that you will find is often included in halloumi itself. I've tried many versions since Yiayia's, where people combine the flavours and add their own herbs and spices, but there is something beautiful about Yiayia's purist versions – her *halloumopites* really let the flavour and texture of the halloumi sing and stand out.

Yiayia Martha moved to the UK in the late 1950s with my *bapou*, Taki, and went on to have two children, the eldest being my dad Marios and the youngest my aunt Androulla. A seamstress by trade, Yiayia turned her hand to many jobs over the years with the main one being our family restaurant, Dirlandas, which they opened in the late 1960s. It was a loud, homely, heartfelt taverna, which they ran for 27 years. It was filled with heart, good food and loyal customers. Yiayia and Bapou lived upstairs, and our lives revolved around that building on Tufnell Park Road.

In the mid-1990s they tried moving back to Cyprus for a gentler way of life (Bapou going back to barbering and Yiayia to dressmaking) but Yiayia's heart wasn't in it. She wanted to be near us, her immediate family.

So they came back. Bapou continued to barber. Yiayia worked on wedding dresses in their little North London flat. And it was (and still is) during these years that I learned and continue to learn from Yiayia. I'd get a phone call to tell me that her friend from church has brought her tender young vine leaves and to go round immediately for *koupepia* (Cypriot stuffed vine leaves), or that it was time she taught me to make *koupes* (bulgur wheat stuffed with meat); I treasure these days and times with her and there will always, always, be some sort of *pita* to eat while we work and talk.

A note on the dried mint: we always have bunches of mint from the garden drying, as it is such a quintessential flavour in Cypriot cooking. Just tie together and hang springs of mint upside down in a cool, dark spot. I use a handful of these leaves in this recipe, but if you can only get the jarred dried ones then 1–2 tablespoons is fine.

Makes 8 buns
Vegetarian

500 g (1 lb 2 oz /4 cups) strong
  white bread flour, plus extra
  for dusting
1 teaspoon sea salt flakes, plus
  extra for sprinkling
1 x 7 g (scant 1 tablespoon) sachet
  active dry yeast
1 tablespoon caster (superfine)
  sugar
300 ml (10 fl oz/1¼ cups)
  warm water
2 tablespoons extra virgin olive
  oil, plus extra for greasing and
  drizzling
large handful of dried mint leaves
  (or 1–2 tablespoons; see intro
  opposite)
½ teaspoon dried oregano
200 g (7 oz) halloumi, chopped into
  cubes
3 tablespoons sesame seeds

Put the flour into a large bowl and stir in the salt.

In a measuring jug (pitcher), whisk the yeast and sugar with the warm water. Leave for 5 minutes, then whisk this mixture into the flour along with the olive oil. Crush in the dried mint leaves, add the dried oregano and mix into the dough (adding more water or flour if needed – you don't want it to be too dry, though).

Turn the dough out onto a lightly floured surface and knead for 8–10 minutes until smooth.

Clean out the bowl, pop the dough back in, then cover with a kitchen towel and leave to rise for 1–1½ hours until doubled in size.

When the dough has risen, knock it back and fold in the chopped halloumi. Work it until the halloumi is evenly mixed in, then divide the dough into eight pieces and shape into balls.

Drizzle a 22 x 33 cm (9 x 13 inches) baking tray (pan) with oil and place the buns in, leaving a bit of room between each one. Leave to rise again for 30 minutes. Meanwhile, preheat the oven to 180°C (400°F/gas 6).

When the buns are ready, sprinkle over the sesame seeds and bake in the oven for 30–35 minutes until golden and cooked through. I like to finish them with a little more extra virgin olive oil and sea salt. Wait patiently (if you can), then tuck in.

YIAYIA VALI'S SMOKY AUBERGINE-STUFFED
TOMATOES FROM ATHENS

Vali lives in the fancy northern Athenian suburb of Kifissia, in a home painted bright yellow to match her personality. There are books everywhere I look – including my own, *Grand Dishes* – and an entire cupboard dedicated to cookbooks. As I step back in time into her kitchen with its 1970s tiles and coral cupboards, she apologises profusely, and I have no idea why. I love a retro kitchen.

Perhaps owing to her stints living abroad, Vali is experimental in the kitchen. This dish borrows from her heritage in Constantinople (modern-day Istanbul), taking inspiration from *hünkar beğendi* or 'sultan's delight', a smoked aubergine (eggplant) and cheese dish in a tomato sauce. The inclusion of butter and cream and the creation of a roux nods to Vali's time in France. This rich dish is best served with a light leaf salad and a crisp glass of Assyrtiko wine.

Makes 8 stuffed tomatoes
Vegetarian

1 kg (2 lb 4 oz) aubergines
  (eggplants)
8 medium to large tomatoes
1 tablespoon olive oil
1½ teaspoons salt, plus extra
  as needed
50 g (2 oz) unsalted butter
50 g (2 oz/scant ½ cup) plain
  (all-purpose) flour
200 ml (7 fl oz/scant 1 cup) single
  (light) cream
1 egg
2 heaped tablespoons grated
  graviera or Parmesan, plus
  extra for sprinkling
sugar

Preheat the oven to 200°C (425°F/gas 7).

Char the aubergines by placing them over an open flame on a gas hob (stovetop) or on the barbecue until soft. Vali adds a sheet of foil under the ring to catch any falling pieces of charred aubergine skin. You'll need to reposition them a few times so that the entire aubergine receives a generous blast of heat and its entire skin is charred. Allow to cool, then peel off the charred skins and chop the flesh and transfer to a sieve to drain out any remaining moisture.

Next, prepare the tomatoes by slicing off the tops (reserve the tops), scooping out the middle and setting the flesh aside in a separate bowl. Sprinkle a little salt and sugar in the bottom of each tomato.

Pour the tomato flesh into a food processor and blitz until smooth, then add the olive oil and ½ teaspoon of the salt and set aside.

In a saucepan, melt the butter over a low heat. Add the flour and whisk fast to combine and create a paste. Quickly add the chopped aubergine as soon as the butter and flour have combined, stirring for a further 1–2 minutes before pouring in the cream. Season with the remaining salt and continue to whisk until you have a thick, creamy filling. Then take off the heat and whisk in the egg, followed by the cheese.

Fill the tomatoes with the aubergine cream, placing their lids on top and pouring in the blitzed tomato flesh you set aside earlier. Then sprinkle with a final grating of cheese.

Bake for 30–40 minutes until the tomatoes are browning on top. If the tomatoes are getting a little too brown on top, cover with kitchen foil and remove it again for the last 5 minutes of baking.

YIAYIA VALI

Born Athens, 1930

'With cooking, sometimes things just come to my mind and I want to try them. I don't make only Greek food. My yiayia and my mother had a very good hand for food. They'd make something and everyone would run to try it. We ate the simplest things during the war, but my yiayia and mother still managed to make them delicious.

During the occupation, we were hungry. They were strange days. Once I went out into the street and a mortar just happened to fall out of the sky next to me. One day, my brother went to the bakery and a group of hungry kids stole everything he had been sent to bring home to us. That's how hungry people were. Children were forced to steal to feed themselves.

Just before the war we had a live-in German nanny so I learned German from her, but it seems she was on the wrong side because before the war really took off, she packed up all of her things and fled back to Germany. Then once Hitler came into power my mother burnt all the German books we had, such was her apathy towards what was happening. Since then, though, I've been able to pick up languages quite easily. We then had a French governess and I went to France in my twenties, so I speak French well and my English is also pretty good because I read a lot.

One lesson in life that I think is very important is to admit to your mistakes, even the mistakes you haven't made. It's good to become softer as you get older – forgive, forget and help others to do the same, even if you feel that you weren't in the wrong in the first place.'

YIAYIA RENA'S SOUGANIA (STUFFED ONIONS) FROM LESVOS

Without ever having met me, Rena's granddaughters have kindly offered to host me in their grand old house in Mytilene, giving an insight into their grandmother's aptitude towards *filoxenia* (the Greek concept of showing kindness to strangers).

What strikes me the most about Lesvos' capital is its architecture: enormous houses with jutting second floors and turrets that I can't compare to anywhere else I've travelled to. It's far from the white-washed cubes with blue shuttered windows you expect to find on Greek islands.

At Rena's, greeted with homemade lemonade and copious excited licks from Takis, her mop-haired dog, I'm treated to a history lesson as well as a meze dish I've never had before. *Sougania*, served with a glass of Lesvos' prime export, ouzo, balances sweet and salty flavours perfectly. Ultra-fine onion layers are wrapped delicately around a spicy, herbed meat filling, which we eat in the dappled shade of Rena's garden after a languid day of swimming. We eat these as a meze, picking up each stuffed onion with a toothpick and swilling it down with the ouzo, but I'm also partial to a blob of yoghurt or sour cream on the side of this one.

Serves 8–10

1 kg (2 lb 4 oz) white onions
3 spring onions (scallions), roughly chopped
½ bunch of parsley
350 g (12 oz) minced (ground) beef
95 g (3¼ oz/scant ½ cup) medium-grain white rice (Rena uses Greek karolina rice, but you can also use arborio)
1 teaspoon salt, plus extra for cooking the onions
½ teaspoon ground cumin
pinch of ground black pepper
100 ml (3½ fl oz/scant ½ cup) extra virgin olive oil
250 ml (8½ fl oz/1 cup) vegetable stock

To prepare the onions, top and tail them and peel the skin off. With a sharp knife, slice into the onion from the side vertically until you reach its core, so you have cut halfway through.

Add the onions to a large saucepan of cool water along with a pinch of salt and bring to the boil. Boil for 4–5 minutes until the onions have softened a little without losing their shape. Drain the water (you can use the onion liquid for your stock if you're using a cube), and set the onions aside to cool while you prepare the filling.

To make the filling, blitz the spring onion whites, half the spring onion greens and the parsley (stalks and all) in a mini chopper, or simply chop very finely. Tip into a large bowl.

Add the beef to the bowl, followed by the rice, salt, cumin, pepper and half of the olive oil. Use a wooden spoon to combine.

Now fill your onion layers. Use the line you sliced into the onion as a starting point and peel off a layer of the onion and fill it with the meat mixture. How much you fill it with will depend on how large your onion layer is. You want the onion to be able to wrap itself fully around the filling, so don't be tempted to fill it too full.

Once it's filled, place it in a large saucepan or casserole dish (Dutch oven) and continue with the same method, adding the filled onions to the pan cut side down and layering them one on top of the other once they take up the entire base. When you get to the smaller inner onion layers, you can fill one, then wrap the gap with another of the smaller onion layers. For the very tiny, unstuffable onion centres, you can either discard them or finely chop them and add them to the filling. Keep going like this until you've used up all the onions and filling.

Pour the vegetable stock into the pan with the remaining olive oil. The stock should come three-quarters of the way up the onions, so top up with a little more stock if needed.

Place a plate on top of the filled onions – Yiayia Rena uses a plate that slots into the pot and acts as a weight on top of the onions so that they don't jump around and come apart as they cook. Don't put a lid on the pan as it stops the stock and juices reducing to make a lovely sauce.

Bring to the boil, then turn down the heat to medium and simmer for 25 minutes until the meat is cooked through and the rice is tender. The onions should look plump, with pale translucent skin and the stock will have reduced right down. Test one for doneness before serving.

YIAYIA RENA

Born Athens, 1938

'We make this dish in Lesvos specifically, but we can't attribute it to the island alone. Its origins are Turkey and further east. All of our stuffed vegetable dishes come from that way. Our influences on the island are really quite mixed: Asia Minor, Greece, Turkey, Ottoman, we're all a confusing and interesting blend.

My house was built in 1740 for a family named Vasileiou. This Vasilieiou had five daughters and he built a house for each of them. The girl that got this house married a man named Kapsymali, another of the "big" and prosperous families on the island.

Our family had houses opposite in Turkey, and we had an olive mill and a soap factory. Another portion of the family had cotton fields in Egypt. We were all spread out at one point. In 1880 Lesvos was a centre for trade. Olive oil, soaps and cotton left here for Europe, Russia, Turkey, Egypt and the Black Sea. Around the end of the 19th century the American cottons had a disease, so everyone began buying cotton from Egypt. Being between East and West, Mytilene was at the heart of the trade and became a very affluent place. It's why we have such distinct architecture here.

Despite being built by Turkish workmen, our grand houses feature lots of windows, unlike the old Turkish homes. Religion didn't permit Muslim women to show themselves so there were far fewer windows in the homes of the people on the Turkish mainland.

The Greeks were quite cunning in getting around building regulations set by the Ottoman Empire. They'd be given permission to build a house to a certain number of square metres, but they'd build out much wider on second and third floors, opening up the space by one metre all the way around the circumference of the building. That's why you see so many strangely shaped houses in Mytilene.'

YIAYIA MARGARITA'S HORIATIKI (VILLAGE SALAD) FROM SANTORINI

Arriving at Margarita's is like stepping into a Santorini frozen in time before tourists descended and made this one of the most visited islands in all of Greece. Based in the south of the island, a good 40-minute drive from the town of Oia (packed with selfie sticks and tourists trying to get the ultimate sunset shots of the iconic sloping caldera), Margarita and her husband live alone in a house on a hill. It overlooks a red beach that hints at the island's explosive volcanic history.

The bleating of goats greets me. Margarita has a ton of animals that roam the periphery of her home. Horses with chestnut manes that gleam in the sun. Chickens and roosters. Dogs that wind between our legs as we prepare lunch at an outdoor table, the inky Aegean Sea our backdrop. She chops our village salad directly into the bowl she serves it in, not caring about making it look delicious but doing so regardless. There's little need for pomp and food styling; the produce here speaks for itself.

'The local tomatoes here are the best in all of Greece,' she tells me, explaining that the volcanic soil makes for hardy produce. 'We barely need to water our tomatoes, it's the ground that feeds them.' What makes this Greek salad extra special is the addition of capers and caper leaves, an extra touch you'll find across the Cycladic islands. The *pièce de résistance* is a huge chunk of feta cheese – doorstep wedge if possible – teetering atop the salad.

Serves 4
Vegetarian

2 large vine tomatoes, roughly chopped
1 small cucumber, peeled and roughly chopped
1 small red onion, finely sliced
1 green (bell) pepper, finely sliced into rings
1 tablespoon caper leaves
1 tablespoon capers
handful of kalamata olives
200 g (7 oz) feta
1 teaspoon dried oregano
olive oil, for dressing the salad

Combine the tomatoes, cucumber and red onion in a bowl.

Top with the green pepper, caper leaves and capers, kalamata olives, then the wedge of feta.

Sprinkle with oregano and add a generous glug of olive oil.

YIAYIA MARGARITA

Born Santorini, 1953

'Even though I was from a big family, my father worked hard enough so that we each got a portion of land, and I've been able to grow my own produce thanks to the portion of land he gave me. From the house we can see Akrotiri, the archaeological site that sadly most of the tourists miss when they come to Santorini.

People don't really know it but it's the Greek Pompeii and it was discovered when I was just a little girl. They found this prehistoric settlement that had been completely covered by ash from the volcano. My father actually knew the archaeologist that found it. Marinatos, his name was˙

My father happened to be out fishing one day and offered Marinatos some *tomatokeftedes* he'd taken with him. From that day on, he'd visit him on the archaeological site where he was working and bring food to him. That was where the idea came from to open a taverna near the site. It's still there – The Cave of Nikolas is what we called it.'

YIAYIA DESPINA'S WHITEBAIT KEFTEDES (FRITTERS) FROM SYMI

Yiayia Despina is someone who puts people instantly at ease. I arrived at her village on the island of Symi in the Dodecanese flustered. The full force of Greek summer is upon us and I'm six months pregnant. She pulls me in for a kiss and squeezes my hand. I ask for a glass of water and she responds, 'Only if it's just the one. Don't go asking for another.' The dry humour and subsequent cackles punctuate our entire afternoon together. I give as good as I get and we're soon best buds.

She lives in the village of Pedi, a small cluster of houses on the waterfront, mirrored by bobbing fishing boats. The entire island only has 3,000 inhabitants, but Despina assures me she keeps herself entertained, despite her quiet existence. 'If you can't have a laugh in life, what do you have?' she says. She's full of brilliant lines like this, pearls of wisdom that she drops in the odd moment of quiet. Another one I love is, 'If you can do something good, do it. If you can't do something good, then don't do something bad, at least.'

The inhabitants of Symi have long relied on their fishing boats to sustain them and fish fritters are what local fishermen make to use up the small fish caught in their nets. You can also make these using fresh anchovies or sardines, too, just remove their heads, tails, spines and innards, and chop them into quarters.

Spiked with spearmint and satisfyingly crispy, these work well as part of a seafood meze. I like to pair them with a Santorini Village Salad (see page 76) and always eat them while they're hot.

Serves 8–10 (makes about 40–45 fritters)

800 g (1 lb 12 oz) fresh whitebait (or anchovies or sardines, gutted and heads and tails removed)
1 teaspoon salt
3 tomatoes
1 onion, coarsely grated
2 eggs, beaten
80 ml (2¾ fl oz/⅓ cup) beer (lager)
80 g (3 oz) graviera or Parmesan, grated
2 teaspoons dried thyme
bunch of fresh mint (Despina uses spearmint, but peppermint is fine too), leaves picked and finely chopped
handful of fresh parsley, leaves finely chopped
1 teaspoon ground black pepper
290 g (10¼ oz/2⅓ cups) plain (all-purpose) flour
2 teaspoons baking powder
600 ml (20 fl oz/2½ cups) sunflower oil

The night before making the *keftedes*, Place the fish in a bowl and sprinkle over the salt. Cover and refrigerate.

Grate the tomatoes into a large bowl, juice, skin and all. Chop any pieces of skin left at the end up and add them in too with the onion.

If you're using fish larger than whitebait, slice the flesh away and remove the spines, then chop the flesh into quarters.

Into the tomato bowl, add the fish, eggs, beer, cheese, herbs and pepper. Stir to combine.

In a separate bowl, combine the flour and baking powder, then add the dry ingredients to the fish and herbs, ensuring everything is well combined and wet.

In a large, deep dry frying pan (skillet) or wok, heat the oil over a medium-high heat. After a minute or so, when the oil is hot (when a tiny bit of the mix sizzles in the oil), take a large tablespoon-size scoop of the *keftedes* mixture and drop it into the hot oil. It should bubble and sizzle but not break apart. If it does break apart, then either the oil isn't hot enough yet or you've taken too big a scoop.

Fry the fritters in batches for 1–2 minutes on each side until golden brown. Once cooked, drain on paper towels and repeat.

Serve the fritters while they're still hot.

YIAYIA DESPINA

Born Samos, 1941

'Both my father and mother would fish to sustain our family. They'd both go out on the boat together and my mother would work just as hard as my father. We've always had strong women in this family. I was actually born while my parents were on the run. The story goes that my parents and older siblings left in a small rowing boat with only a few possessions. They had no idea where they might be heading, only that they needed to get away from Symi immediately.

During the war years, practically the entire island fled because we were occupied by the Italians and so it turned out that I came into the world on the island of Samos, not Symi. Then from Samos we crossed over to Turkey and for the first few years of my life, we lived in Palestine and in Beirut. I obviously don't remember much of that time, but I know that we were an enclave of Greeks from the most eastern islands who had fled Europe and gone further east in order not to be embroiled in the war. My first language was French, not Greek and I do still remember bits of French, if I hear it being spoken around me.

It wasn't just the Italians and the Germans that were a threat in those days, many on the island were being accused of being communist by our own people – my family included. There was so much civil unrest in Greece for a great portion of my life. Even on an island like Symi, we didn't escape it. I remember the years of the dictatorship, feeling like we couldn't even leave the house without fear of punishment.

Thankfully we live very different lives now and in spite of our proximity to Turkey, we feel stable and safe here. I don't really leave the village, but I don't mind that. We have a laugh here. What else can we do?'

YIAYIA TOULA'S TARAMOSALATA
FROM PALAIO FALIRO

Located on the Athenian coastline in a modernist apartment block in Palaio Faliro, the enormously animated Yiayia Toula offers to cook seafood with me. I've been craving *taramosalata* so when her grandson Jason informs me that she's famous in all the family for her tarama, it seems foretold. While 'fish roe dip' never sounds very appetising, that is exactly what this is. It's miles away from the baby pink stuff you'll find in a supermarket and far tastier. It's also so easy to make that I'll never venture into a shop to buy taramosalata again.

Serves 6

70 g (2½ oz) stale bread (one hefty slice of sourdough should do it)
70 g (2½ oz) white tarama (salted and cured fish roe)
1 lemon
200 ml (7 fl oz/scant 1 cup) corn oil

Soak the bread in a shallow bowl of water for a minute or so before draining and squeezing any extra moisture out of the bread.

Put the tarama and 2 tablespoons of lemon juice in a food processor and blitz until just mixed.

Break up the soaked bread with your hands and add to the food processor, followed by half the corn oil and blitz again until just mixed. Add the rest of the oil and blitz again, then taste and add more lemon juice as needed. If it's a little too fishy for your liking, add a little extra bread and blitz again.

YIAYIA TOULA

Born Amfissa, 1927

'On Kathari Deftera (Clean Monday), the first day of Orthodox Lent, Greek families gather to eat a big spread of taramosalata, calamari, octopus and shellfish. In our family there's always a huge feast at this time of year and of course, I like to take a big box full of tarama as my contribution. Even if there's other taramosalata on the table, it usually won't be touched. They all wait for me to arrive and say "Yiayia Toula, your tarama is the best one."

I live on the coast so I eat a lot of seafood. I moved to Athens from Amfissa in my early twenties and learned to make *saganaki* after I was married. We would eat meze at a little taverna here on the coast and prawn *saganaki* would always feature, so I began making it at home.

I had a *proxenio* (arranged marriage). My sister had arranged for me to go and meet him because he was looking for a wife and he worked with my sister's husband. He was nearing 40 and I was 22. I saw him from afar and he didn't make much of an impression. I loved him, I didn't fall in love with him. For a year before we married, every Tuesday he would leave Palaio Faliro and come to see me in Amfissa. Slowly, slowly, I started to care for him. There's a difference between *agapi* (love) and *erotas* (passion). *Erotas* comes and goes. *Agapi* remains. Erotas is for, you know, sex. That's all. It's love that remains.'

YIAYIA TOULA'S PRAWN SAGANAKI
FROM PALAIO FALIRO

Inside the shaded arcades of Athens' central market or down by the port of Piraeus, a diverse collection of characters pop in and out of *mezedopoleio* or *ouzeri* for a quick pick-me-up in the form of a short glass of ouzo or *tsipouro* and a plate of meze. Prawn (shrimp) *saganaki* is a classic in the city and one that Yiayia Toula, having lived by the sea in Palaio Faliro, knows well. The rich tomato sauce, suffused with the flavour of prawns and the freshness of spearmint is one you'll want to mop up with a load of crusty bread.

Serves 4

1 kg (2 lb 4 oz) whole shell-on jumbo king prawns (shrimp)
350 g (12 oz) feta, cut into 1 cm (½ inch) thick slices
15 g (½ oz) mint, leaves picked and roughly torn (Toula uses spearmint, but you can use peppermint too)
1 teaspoon cracked black pepper
4 tomatoes, sliced
100 ml (3½ fl oz/scant ½ cup) extra virgin olive oil
crusty bread, to serve

Preheat the oven to 180°C (400°F/gas 6).

Gently peel the legs and shell from the prawns, leaving the tail and head intact (these have lots of flavour). Devein the prawns by gently running a knife along the top of the prawn and pulling out the dark 'string'. No need to go too deep for this, it's just under the surface.

Layer the prawns in a deep baking dish. Follow this with a layer of the sliced feta (don't worry if the slices break up), then the mint leaves. Add the black pepper (Toula says there's no need for salt, there's enough in the feta).

Finally, add the sliced tomatoes, completely covering the mint leaves below so they don't burn in the oven. Tuck the mint leaves behind the tomatoes if they are sticking out.

Drizzle over the olive oil and bake in the oven for 40 minutes until the tomatoes have broken down and become a bit saucy. If you don't have super-ripe Mediterranean tomatoes they may sit on top more, but don't worry, it will still be delicious.

Serve hot with crusty bread for dipping.

YIAYIA MARY'S DOLMADAKIA (STUFFED VINE LEAVES) FROM KASOS

Perhaps one of the most remote Greek islands I've ever had the pleasure of visiting, Kasos is a bumpy boat ride away from Karpathos. The ferry doesn't run every day on account of there being so few residents on the island, so I have to time my visit to Yiayia Mary with just the right weather conditions that will allow the *Kasos Princess* to get me there.

The island may be small, but it's rugged, with sun-scorched mountain passes that lead up into the hills from Kasos' tiny harbour. Up there I find hundreds of goats, the odd monastery and a fiery sunset that lights up the entire landscape.

Yiayia Mary lives down in the village with her husband. She cooks in an outdoor garden and a smile never leaves her face as we roll these teeny tiny *dolmades* during golden hour. The island has a reputation for making the smallest dolmades in all of Greece, hence the diminutive *dolmadakia*, meaning 'small dolmades.'

Makes about 35 *dolmadakia*

250 g (9 oz) minced (ground) beef
1 onion, finely chopped
85 g (3 oz/scant ½ cup) short-grain
  rice (Mary uses glacé rice, but you
  can use pudding or risotto rice)
60 g (2 oz) tomato purée (paste)
65 g (2¼ oz) unsalted butter, plus
  1 tablespoon to finish
½ teaspoon cracked black pepper
1 teaspoon sea salt flakes
300 g (10½ oz) preserved vine
  leaves
juice of 1 lemon

In a large bowl, break up the beef, then combine with all the remaining ingredients except the vine leaves, extra butter and lemon juice, to make the *dolmadakia* filling.

Prepare the vine leaves by stacking them up and cutting away any tough stalks with scissors. Yiayia Mary used very small vine leaves she preserved herself, but most shop-bought ones will be bigger.

Take one leaf at a time and place it on your surface (shiny side down and veiny side up). Yiayia Mary used ½ teaspoon of filling per leaf, but for larger leaves use a heaped teaspoon. Place the filling at the bottom of the leaf in the centre, where the stalk used to join. Neaten and shape the filling into a slight sausage shape with your fingers and then fold the bottom of the leaf up and over the filling, folding the sides inwards as you go. Continue to roll up, keeping everything nice and tight and when done, place it in a large, lidded saucepan, join-side down. Repeat with the remaining filling and leaves. Discard any torn leaves as you go.

Once you have used up all the filling, make sure that the *dolmadakia* are tightly packed side by side in the saucepan (this will stop them moving around too much during cooking). It's fine to stack them in two layers if needed.

Add the extra tablespoon of butter and top the *dolmadakia* with a heavy plate that fits neatly into the saucepan, acting as a weight that will prevent them from moving around as they cook. Pour in enough water to just cover the *dolmadakia*, squeeze in the lemon juice, then bring to a boil. Reduce the heat to medium and simmer with the lid on for about 20 minutes, or until cooked through. Once cooked, carefully drain and reserve the liquid from the saucepan, holding firmly down on the plate so as not to dislodge any of the dolmadakia. Keep this stock for something else like a simple soup, as it's very tasty, and transfer the dolmadakia to a serving dish, tightening any loosened leaves back up.

Serve hot or cold. Yiayia Mary serves hers as a meze, with fresh apricots from the garden and local cheese from Kasos.

YIAYIA MARY

Born Kasos, 1951

'My mother was actually born in Egypt and she met my father there. Many people from Kasos lived in Egypt in the early 1900s because of the Suez Canal and the jobs it offered. It was a prosperous place to live at the time.

For Greeks of my generation the place to go was America. So we emigrated, and for a while we lived in the States. Imagine, we left Kasos, this tiny island, in the 1970s and ended up in the Bronx. I didn't like it at all and can't say I made many friends. I didn't speak the language and I had young children, so I stayed at home to raise them. I do regret that I didn't make the most of my time there. I once had an offer to go to the Caribbean from a family we knew there, but I didn't take them up on it.

Nowhere compares to Kasos, it's very special. We might be a small island, but we have our own traditions and identity here. Even the *dolmadakia* we make here are specific to the island. We make them particularly small, smaller than your little finger.

In advance of the *panigiri* on 15 August (celebrating the Assumption of Mary) all the women in the neighbourhood will get together in the village square outside of the church and spend hours rolling *dolmadakia*. The band will start playing music in advance of the party as we prepare the food and it's been like this since I was a little girl. It's a long process, rolling so many *dolma*, but when you have good company and music, it becomes a part of the party. Then we eat, dance and sing until the following morning.'

YIAYIA MARIETTA'S SUFIKO (VEGETABLE MEDLEY) FROM IKARIA

Marietta looks two decades younger than her years. There isn't a line on her face, but this apparently is standard in Ikaria, the 'island of longevity', upon which locals live to a much riper old age.

I drive past a beach full of young surfers, up through herds upon herds of goats and into the hills of this special island, to a village shaded by lush plane trees to find Marietta, who welcomes me with a shot of her own home-made alcohol. It's 10 a.m. and within ten minutes we're dancing a rhythmic Ikariotiko folk dance around the taverna that she runs with her son.

What keeps her so fresh? She swears by sex, a bit of what you fancy (meaning wine whenever you want it) and dancing. I suspect her veggie-dense diet might also have something to do with it but I'm happy to give the other elixirs of life a try too.

This *sufiko* brings together a range of summer vegetables from the garden, along with olive oil and wine – essentials in the Ikarian diet. It's a bit like a Sicilian caponata, slick and shiny in its oily sauce, but with plenty more veg thrown in for extra measure. It's just as good cold as it is hot, making it a great side at a barbecue or an ideal addition to a picnic.

Serves 4
Vegan

100 ml (3½ fl oz/scant ½ cup)
  extra virgin olive oil
2 red onions, finely sliced into
  half-moons
1 large courgette (zucchini), cut
  into 2.5 cm (1 inch) cubes
2 medium aubergines (eggplants),
  cut into 2.5 cm (1 inch) cubes
400 g (14 oz) pumpkin or sweet
  potato, cut into 2.5 cm (1 inch)
  cubes
2 red (bell) peppers, cubed
2 green (bell) peppers, cubed
1 tablespoon salt
ladleful of water
2 large tomatoes, chopped
5 garlic cloves
handful of chopped parsley leaves
100 ml (3½ fl oz/scant ½ cup)
  red wine
bread, to serve

Heat the oil in a deep frying pan (skillet) or wok with a lid over a medium heat and fry the onions for 1 minute, then add the courgettes, aubergines and pumpkin or sweet potato, stirring so that none of the vegetables stick to the pan.

Once the aubergines begin to soften a little, add the peppers and salt and the water, then cover the pan with the lid and allow the vegetables to steam.

In the meantime, blend the tomatoes with the garlic in a food processor, then add this to the pan with the parsley, stirring to combine.

Add the red wine and simmer over a medium-high heat for 20 minutes, or until the water cooks off and you're left with slick and shiny vegetables.

Serve with bread (and wine), as per Marietta's strict instructions.

YIAYIA MARIETTA

Born Ikaria, 1943

'A doctor in Athens once didn't believe my age when I told him. He had the cheek to ask me if I still have sex and I thought, "What a question!" But really, it's true. It does keep you feeling young if you're still active in that department. Psychologically, sex helps.

People come here and ask what the secret is to our eternal youth but there isn't one answer we can give. Maybe it's good genes, maybe it's our lifestyle. I'm not a doctor, but I can say that life here is different because we have our own produce, and we grow without pesticides and all the sprays they use on vegetables to feed the masses. Maybe having your own garden with your own vegetables helps?

One absolute misconception about us Ikarians is that we don't work. It's not true. We work hard and we all have jobs to do. The difference is that in Ikaria, we're not on a schedule like everywhere else. If we've been dancing all night at the *panigiri*, we'll tend to our goats and sheep directly afterwards at sunrise. People come and comment that we're not out in the fields, but we're doing it before they even wake up! We live life on our own time and that's the greatest freedom of all.'

YIAYIA ELEUTERIA'S DAKOS SALAD FROM CRETE

Dakos is a dish made with *paximadi*, a Cretan rusk traditionally made with barley, salt and sourdough. It forms the base of this idiosyncratic dish from the island that to me, toes the line between salad and something else entirely. One story I've heard about the humble beginnings of *paximadia* is that Cretan fishermen would take the rusks, twice baked by their wives to endure the wet and wavy weather, out at sea. They'd dunk the crunchy, circular rusk into the waves before topping it with tomato, feta and olives, allowing the rusk to soften a little before diving in.

Yiayia Eleuteria, who heads up the kitchen at Lambros Taverna in the sun-soaked village of Tertsa, prefers to splash her own rusks with water before adding a generous topping of locally grown, salted tomatoes. Enjoy this one as a side to her roast lamb (see page 160) or as part of a Greek meze selection. Top it with enough feta and you've made a satisfying salad you can enjoy solo.

Serves 1
Vegetarian

1 large, circular rusk
1 tomato, grated (do not drain the juices!)
200 g (7 oz) feta, crumbled
30 ml (2 tablespoons) olive oil
handful of kalamata olives
dried oregano
sea salt flakes

Prepare the rusk by rinsing it for 2 seconds under the tap.

Place the rusk in a shallow bowl and top with the tomato, followed be a sprinkling of sea salt flakes. Add the feta, followed by the olive oil. Top with the olives and a final sprinkling of oregano.

YIAYIA NITSA'S GIGANTES (OVEN-BAKED BUTTER BEANS) FROM THESSALONIKI

In Thessaloniki, I binge on the local pastry *bougatsa*, this one filled with semolina, for breakfast and I'm already bursting at the seams by the time I get to Nitsa's. I do tell her this, but she insists on feeding me mini Papadopoulos chocolates in a royal blue wrapper and won't allow me to stand after discovering I'm pregnant.

Like her baked *gigantes*, Nitsa is an absolute comfort. She floats effortlessly across the kitchen, whipping bits out of the refrigerator, chopping onion directly into a vast pot and knocking up Greek coffees for her friend and photographer Marco in between. She throws together the ingredients so swiftly, I barely have time to register what she's done.

This tomato-rich dish that sings of spearmint is one that can be enjoyed piping hot, simply with a hunk of bread or chunk of feta in winter. Or, in summer, add it to a meze selection and serve it at room temperature. The key is to always soak your beans the night before and keep an eye on them to ensure they're not drying out in the oven.

Serves 4–5
Vegan

500 g (1 lb 2 oz/2½ cups) dried butter (lima) beans, soaked overnight
1 tablespoon salt, plus extra as needed
200 ml (7 fl oz/scant 1 cup) olive oil
2 onions, roughly chopped
1 red (bell) pepper, chopped
1 red chilli, chopped
3 garlic cloves, roughly chopped
1 teaspoon ground pepper
½ bunch of spearmint, leaves chopped
½ bunch of parsley, chopped (including the stalks)
3 large tomatoes, grated into a bowl (add a tablespoon of tomato purée/paste if they're not in season and looking a little anaemic, or replace the tomatoes with 400 g/14 oz good-quality passata/sieved tomatoes)
700 ml (24 fl oz/scant 3 cups) water

Drain the soaked beans, rinse them thoroughly in a sieve, then add them to a large saucepan.

Cover with cold water, add the salt, then bring to the boil. Reduce the heat to medium and simmer for 1¼ hours.

In a separate pan, heat the oil over a medium heat and fry the onions, red pepper, chilli and garlic for 10 minutes before adding in the herbs and seasoning with salt.

Add the tomatoes or passata and allow the sauce to cook down for a further 5 minutes before removing from the heat.

Preheat the oven to 200°C (425°F/gas 7).

Once the beans are cooked, drain them and add them to a baking tray (pan) or casserole dish (Dutch oven). Pour over the sauce. Mix well, then top up with the water.

Cover the beans with a lid or kitchen foil and bake in the oven for 30 minutes. After this time, check the beans – if they are looking a little dry, splash in a little more water. Remove the lid or foil and bake for a further 30 minutes until the beans are soft and the sauce is reduced.

YIAYIA NITSA

Born Florina, 1944

'My husband always said that any dinner table should always have a serving of *gigantes* on it, no matter what you're eating. We make *gigantes* in the north of Greece because it gets chilly up here, and it sees us through winter. I was actually born further north in Florina, where we are famous for our red peppers, so I make a point of adding a red pepper to my *gigantes*.

I was raised in Thessaloniki and have seen it transform in my lifetime. My own house was one of the first buildings in the neighbourhood. We were surrounded by fields, then slowly but surely, apartment blocks began to spring up around the house.

In 1978 there was an enormous earthquake and this house had to be completely rebuilt. I was inside with my daughter, mother and grandmother and we had to run out without a second to think. The floors and ceiling were cracking and in a split second we ran for it. I'd never experienced anything like it. We watched the house crumble. We ended up living in tents that summer for a couple of months and honestly, it was the best holiday I've ever had.

We have an interesting cultural mix here in Thessaloniki, but some Greeks don't realise that we were once refugees too. I'm Orthodox but I don't believe I'm better than anyone else because of my religion. I read that the Greek priests are condemning yoga now because it's the work of the devil. Where do they even get these things from?'

YIAYIA MEROPI'S KOLOKITHI PAPOUTSAKIA (STUFFED COURGETTES) FROM LESVOS

Incredibly rural with minimal tourism, Lesvos feels like the Greece of old. The island sits so close to Turkey that I can see the mainland. To get to Yiayia Meropi, I drive around a coastal road that leads into sleepy villages where locals disappear come mesimeri (the midday siesta hours). Her home has a view over the Gulf of Kalloni and we cook out on her veranda, a soundtrack of bees and cicadas for company.

A twist on the traditional rice-filled tomato and pepper dish, yemista, Yiayia Meropi's papoutsakia (meaning little shoes) work well as part of a summer meze spread. If you want to make this dish vegan, simply omit the eggs and cheese, replacing the cheese with the same weight of breadcrumbs or roughly chopped walnuts for extra crunch.

Serves 4–6
Vegetarian

2 kg (4 lb 8 oz) large courgettes (zucchini)
4 teaspoons salt
100 ml (3½ fl oz/scant ½ cup) extra virgin olive oil, plus extra for drizzling
4 onions, blitzed or grated
650 g (1 lb 7 oz) tomatoes, chopped
½ teaspoon ground black pepper
1 green (bell) pepper, finely chopped
bunch of parsley, leaves finely chopped
3 eggs
150 g (5 oz) graviera or Parmesan, grated, plus extra to finish

Preheat the oven to 200°C (425°F/gas 7) and line a baking tray (pan) with baking parchment.

Prepare the courgettes by slicing them in half lengthways, then make an indentation of around 2 cm (¾ inch) with a sharp knife on the inside of each one, following the curve at the end of the courgette. Place the courgettes in a wide saucepan, flesh side down, and sprinkle over 2 teaspoons of the salt, then pour in enough water to just cover the courgettes. Bring to the boil, then immediately reduce the heat to low and simmer for 10 minutes. This will make the flesh of the courgettes easier to scoop out.

Drain the courgettes and allow to cool, then scoop out the flesh with a teaspoon (reserve the flesh), placing your empty courgette halves on the prepared baking tray.

Put the reserved courgette flesh in a colander over a bowl to drain any excess water, or else strain the water out by placing the flesh into a piece of muslin (cheesecloth) and squeezing the moisture out. Once strained, finely chop the flesh.

Heat the oil in a very deep frying pan (skillet) or wide saucepan over a medium heat and fry the onions for 3 minutes, then add the chopped courgette flesh followed by the remaining salt. Fry for a further 3 minutes before adding the tomatoes. Increase the heat to high and cook for 5 minutes, or until the excess liquid from the filling has cooked off. Remove from the heat and leave to cool to room temperature. Once cooled, stir in the remaining ingredients.

Drizzle the courgette halves with olive oil, then use a tablespoon to drop the filling into each one. Top with a further grating of cheese, then bake in the oven for 30 minutes, or until the courgettes are nicely browned on top.

YIAYIA MEROPI

Born Lesvos, 1947

'Lesvos is so close to Turkey that the island's always been a gateway to Europe. We had a huge influx of refugees coming through because of the war in Syria, and Lesvos became the focus of lots of international attention. The people of Lesvos really tried to help at first, but the island's population was up by 25,000 people. We doubled in size. It's not dissimilar to what happened in 1922 when ethnic Greeks living in Turkey had to leave their homes across the water. They came to Lesvos and had to live anywhere they could find, in old sheds and olive mills. We don't realise how lucky we are.'

YIAYIA DESPINA'S FOURTALIA
(EGG AND POTATO OMELETTE) FROM ANDROS

When I ring Yiayia Despina up to arrange our time together in Andros, she calls me 'agapi mou' (my love) without having ever met me. Each time we touch base before I head out to the Cyclades by ferry, she answers the phone and speaks with such warmth that I find myself grinning as she speaks.

Despina lives behind a church in a whitewashed village on the sloping hills of the island that are at this time of year peppered with velvet red poppies. Pots of geraniums line her veranda and the idiosyncratic beaded curtain at the front door hides an absolute cave of wonders inside.

She meets me with a bouquet of freshly picked jasmine, a slice of walnut cake, loukoumia, local cheese, Greek coffee and a carton of juice. This woman likes to indulge her guests. She probably picked up her need to feed while running the village's first supermarket and kafeneion, both of which were once in the house she now lives in. Bobbing from room to room, arms wide in emphasis and eyes clearly lost in another moment in time, she proudly tells me, 'This shelf would be full of preserved meats, we had the bakery downstairs.' In a room now housing a double bed above which are shelves crammed full of religious icons, she says, 'This was the phone centre, where everyone in the village would come to make their phone calls.'

Together with her husband, they ran what became the village hub. Now she lives alone and the village that overlooks the inky Aegean below has only 50 permanent residents. Her home is full in a chaotic but homely way. Crochet, floral prints, embroidered fabrics and plastic fruits fill every nook and cranny of the centuries-old village house. It's the most perfect granny setting, in every way. Photographer Marco can barely drink his coffee for needing to snap away at her rose-print three-piece sofa set.

The fourtalia we make is an Andros classic; a thick wedge of potato omelette that rivals a Spanish tortilla, with extra sprinklings of oregano and spearmint. Despina says that the women in the village call this 'the lazy man's dish', on account of how easy it is to whip up. An omelette it may be, but this yiayia serves hers with village wine and a Greek salad. It's so hearty that it would make for a good go-to dinner. I like to treat myself to this one for Sunday brunch. Don't be tempted to skimp on the oil and butter – the potatoes need it.

Serves 4
Vegetarian

70 ml (2¼ fl oz/generous ¼ cup) extra virgin olive oil
25 g (1 oz) unsalted butter
1 kg (2 lb 4 oz) potatoes, peeled, halved and sliced into 3 mm (⅛ inch) half-moons
1 teaspoon salt
1 teaspoon dried oregano
½ teaspoon dried spearmint
7 eggs
40 ml (1⅓ fl oz/generous 2 tablespoons) whole milk
freshly ground black pepper

Heat the olive oil and butter in a large, deep frying pan (skillet) over a medium-high heat. Once the butter has melted, add the potatoes and sprinkle in the salt, plenty of black pepper and the dried herbs. Cover with a lid and cook for about 15 minutes, stirring occasionally so that they don't stick, until they take on a golden hue.

When the potatoes are ready, crack the eggs into a bowl and whisk in the milk. Pour this mixture over the potatoes and move the saucepan, tilting it in a circular motion so that the egg filters into the gaps between all the potatoes. Cook for 2 minutes, or until the top of the fourtalia is beginning to set.

Yiayia Despina flips the pan with its lid on, so the fourtalia lands onto the lid. She then slides it back into the pan and cooks the other side for a minute. You could stick your pan under the grill for 2 minutes so that the top cooks.

YIAYIA DESPINA

Born Andros, 1937

'Tips for life? One I have for relationships is to hold onto your anger and to not speak it out loud until the fire of the argument has turned to embers. Life isn't just all blue skies. There are ups and downs in relationships and you have to accept that. What I've learned is that women should keep quiet in the heat of the moment. What happened with me and my own husband is I'd keep it inside and wait for him to realise his own mistakes, and he always would. I somehow managed to have the upper hand in that way.

I always had control of things in the home and in our business. I was the bookkeeper and I decided where the money was spent. When we bought our second home in Piraeus, I remember going with a suitcase full of cash to Passalimani to buy the house. Millions of drachmas, notes and notes I'd stuffed in there. Those were different days, when business was booming and I couldn't close the till for the amount of drachmas that spilled out of it.'

Comforting

YIAYIA ANASTASIA'S FAKES (LENTIL SOUP) FROM CORFU

Yiayia seems to always have her own second opinion whenever anyone around her sees a doctor. She grew up one of ten children and didn't see a medical professional until the birth of her first child in Germany. Whenever I refuse food or drink that she offers she'll say, 'Why? Did the doctor order that?' always delivered with great sarcasm and a grim expression.

Hers was an upbringing punctuated with tragedy. Siblings died young. Corfu was occupied by Italians in her formative years and what food they had went to the occupying soldiers first. She learned from a young age that food has the power to heal and has forever put her trust in the land and its produce to remedy.

I make this whenever I'm in need of a pick-me-up, whether it be a cold or a break-up that has driven me to the stove. Garlic has antibiotic properties, and it adds an intense kick to this otherwise humble and easy-to-rustle-up lentil soup. Yiayia is quite indignant when I suggest we cut back on the half a bulb she adds to the recipe, so don't be shy when adding your garlic. We eat ours topped with feta, with a side of salty olives and *dolmades* (stuffed vine leaves).

Serves 4
Vegan

250 g (9oz/1⅓ cups) brown lentils
1 tablespoon salt
40 ml (1⅓ fl oz/generous
   2 tablespoons) extra virgin
   olive oil
½ onion, finely chopped
½ bulb of garlic, cloves finely sliced
½ teaspoon ground black pepper
2 bay leaves
1 tablespoon tomato purée (paste)

First, soak the lentils in warm water for at least 30 minutes.

Drain the lentils into a sieve and rinse them under running water, then add to a saucepan and cover with cold water. You want the water to cover the lentils by about 2.5 cm (1 inch). Add the salt and bring to the boil.

Now throw in the rest of the ingredients (except the tomato purée) and simmer over a low heat for 40 minutes. When there is just 5 minutes left, stir in the tomato purée. If the soup's still looking a bit watery, simmer for a little longer.

YIAYIA POLY'S WINTER FASOLADA (BEAN SOUP) FROM NAXOS

Dedication by Karolos Michailidis, food stylist and recipe developer

Yiayia Poly is the epitome of class and elegance. She's well-mannered, witty and independent. She has always kept a notebook, in which she summarises every dinner party or cards night. She lists the guests, the menu, the table settings she did and what tableware she used. She says that this helps her to avoid repeating things if she hosts the same guests again soon after. Every time she sets the table before a dinner party – always a day or two in advance – she jokingly tells me to take a picture of the table so that when she is not with us anymore I know how to set it correctly, and which plates go with which wine glasses and napkins. It is in these past years that I have realized that my aesthetics and passion for cooking and hosting are derived from Yiayia Poly.

Although born and raised in central Athens, as her mother was too, she has travelled a lot and is a well-informed woman. Even now she cuts out pieces from the newspaper or magazines related to architecture, design or art so she can give them to me to read.

When she got married to my pappou, she didn't know many recipes, but she eventually picked them up by asking her mother or the cook, Harikleia, whom they would hire when hosting formal dinners. Harikleia taught Yiayia many different recipes: crêpes with prawns and avocados, chicken Milanese, choux with different fillings. Yiayia also travelled a lot so took influence from the foods she tasted abroad.

When Yiayia was young, hired cooks with origins in Egypt or France taught housewives like her how to make more international dishes to impress their guests. Over the years, there's been a mixing in Greek cuisine. As Yiayia recalls, before the occupation and evacuation of Smyrna in 1922, Greek cuisine was quite bland. The people who lived in Smyrna and arrived in Greece brought their culture and influenced the evolution and richness of Greek food as we know it today.

One very Greek recipe Yiayia Poly knew how to make from a young age was this *fasolada*, a stew or soup made with white beans. She thinks she learned to make it from a lady who was hired to cook at her house, who was from Naxos. It's perfect winter food: healthy, easy and very comforting. She says that the secret to making the soup thicker and richer is to press and 'melt' some of the beans with your cooking spoon inside the saucpan when the soup is ready. This will give some body to the soup and help it thicken. It is also important to check that the beans you have bought haven't cracked. At the end, she always adds a bit of lemon juice to give the soup a bit of acidity. Yiayia always accompanies the soup with some bread, feta cheese, olives and anchovies or sardines.

Serves 6
Vegan

500 g (1 lb 2 oz/2½ cups) dried
  cannellini beans, soaked
  overnight (you can also use
  tinned beans, see method)
150 ml (5 fl oz/scant ⅔ cup) extra
  virgin olive oil
1 large onion, grated
3–4 carrots, finely chopped
3 celery stalks, finely chopped
1 tablespoon tomato purée (paste),
  or a bit of tomato juice
1 vegetable stock cube
pinch of paprika (Yiayia Poly also
  sometimes uses chilli flakes)
squeeze of lemon juice
salt and freshly ground black
  pepper
bread, to serve

Drain the soaked beans. (If you forgot this step, you can boil the beans in water for 30 minutes and then drain them.)

Heat half the olive oil in a large saucepan over a medium heat, then stir in the vegetables, sautéing for a few minutes before adding the drained beans and sautéing for a further 1 minute.

Add enough water to cover the beans by 1 cm (½ inch), then drop in the stock cube and tomato purée and mix well. Cover and simmer over a medium-low heat for about 1 hour. If you use tinned beans or have pre-boiled them, the cooking time will be 30–35 minutes.

Towards the end of cooking, season with salt, pepper and paprika or chilli flakes and the remaining olive oil. Adding some olive oil at the end of cooking helps retain the flavour and nutritional value of the oil. Boil for a further 10 minutes, then use a spoon to press some of the beans against the pan to 'melt' them and thicken the soup.

Serve the soup hot with bread and a squeeze of lemon juice.

YIAYIA POLY'S GIOUVARLAKIA (MEATBALLS IN TOMATO SAUCE) FROM ATHENS

Traditionally in Greece, soul-soothing *giouvarlakia* are paired with an *avgolemono* (egg and lemon) sauce, but Yiayia Poly is not a purist so she makes a tomato sauce to sit her meatballs in instead. An Athenian yiayia with a modern sensibility and cutting humour that's as sharp as her nose, Poly takes an inventive approach to cooking, looking out beyond Greece for many of her favourite dishes.

It takes us a while to land on a classic Greek dish when discussing what her contribution to this book will be, but there's absolutely no way I'm missing Poly out. She lives in a typical polykatoikia (apartment block) in Athens' well-heeled Kolonaki neighbourhood and is representative of the elegant and refined yiayiades that make up a good portion of the city's population.

We settle on *giouvarlakia* to make together, Poly instructing me to do the jobs she least enjoys (like grating the onion) and pointedly ordering her grandson, Karolos, around, all the while amusing us with her sarcasm and wry wit. She's a force to be dealt with but her warming *giouvarlakia* in this sweet tomato sauce reveal the care and love that she obviously has for her grandchildren. A true yiayia in every sense.

Yiayia Poly serves her *giouvarlakia* with a small tipple of beer (she drinks one small glass every day), crusty bread and hunks of feta.

Serves 6

FOR THE SAUCE
680 g (1 lb 8 oz) passata (sieved tomatoes)
1 vegetable stock cube dissolved in 680 ml (23 fl oz/2¾ cups) water
180 ml (6 fl oz/¾ cup) extra virgin olive oil
1¼ teaspoons freshly ground black pepper
1 teaspoon sugar

FOR THE *GIOUVARLAKIA*
2 red onions, grated
1 kg (2 lb 4 oz) minced (ground) beef
1 large egg
1 teaspoon salt
1 tablespoon ground black pepper
½ bunch of parsley, leaves finely chopped
3 tablespoons long-grain rice
plain (all-purpose) flour, for dusting

In a large saucepan, combine the passata, stock, olive oil, pepper and sugar, then bring to the boil. Cover, reduce the heat to medium and simmer for 15–20 minutes while you prepare the meatballs.

Drain any excess liquid from the grated onions using a piece of muslin (cheesecloth) or a sieve, then transfer to a bowl. Add the beef, egg, salt, pepper, parsley and rice and use your hands to combine.

Pour a little flour onto a plate, ready to coat your meatballs.

Roll the meat mixture into golf-ball-sized-spheres, dipping each meatball into the plate of flour so that it is lightly dusted all over before setting aside on a large plate or tray.

Once you've rolled all the meat into balls, add them to the pot of sauce and ensure they are entirely covered by the liquid. If you need to you can add a dash of water so that the liquid just covers the meatballs. Cover and simmer over a medium heat for 20–30 minutes, or until the sauce has thickened. If it's still on the watery side, simmer uncovered for a little longer.

YIAYIA POLY

Born Athens, 1928

'We've been through so much here in Greece. I've lived through wars and then civil wars. I was part of the National Liberation Front of Greece (the main resistance to the Nazi and Fascist occupation of Greece during the Second World War) when I was a teenager. I didn't even really know what it was, but I was going out to protests just to be going out, to be a part of something. Our lives were so restricted because of the occupation that EAM rallies and meetings became our way of socialising.

I was so young when the war began that when I heard the sirens warning of imminent war with Germany for the first time I was pleased because I wouldn't have to go to school. I lived in Kolonaki then, too, but it was very different to how it is now, there really weren't so many apartment blocks. Old neighbourhoods like Kypseli and Patission were the fancy neighbourhoods back then, the best architects in Greece designed those buildings and the Fokionos Negri esplanade is where we'd go to drink coffee and meet up with friends.

Mount Lycabettus at one point was still full of shepherds and their herds. They'd sell milk in the streets of Kolonaki. Look up the hill now and you'll see these modernist apartment blocks with swimming pools on the roof. Of course, some things still haven't changed. The *laiki* (market) still happens on Xenokratous Street and an eatery that's older than I am, Filippou, is still going strong. They make dishes like these *giouvarlakia* – homely Greek food.'

YIAYIA SOFIA'S MAGIRIO
(SUMMER VEGETABLE STEW) FROM IKARIA

To get to Sofia's coffee shop in Vrakades, I drive around winding coastal bends, sensing the wild energy of the island. Rugged mountains jut into romantic wisps of cloud and white sand beaches are lapped at by crashing waves powered by the Aegean's famous north wind, the *meltemi*. Pine-surrounded villages like Raches spill with activity. Locals play backgammon with gusto for hours under the dappled shade. In verdant valleys, shepherds herd goats and vineyards are plucked at for their purple bounty. Ikaria is an island very much alive, in spite of its reputation for its islanders' laid-back way of life. By night, wild local festivals see traditional stone villages fill with the thrum of a drum, the heart-whipping strings of the violin and dancing. Endless dancing.

Conviviality is the Ikarian way. At Sofia's *kafeneion*, friends drift in and out over the course of a day, nursing a silty Greek coffee for hours. After feeding the goats, we prepare lunch together while people continue to drop by. This *magirio* is a simple veggie stew that demands prime produce. Only the best olive oil and vegetables will do for a dish that depends on a tasty combination of organic, seasonal ingredients for its flavour.

Serves 4
Vegan

150 ml (5 fl oz/scant ⅔ cup) water
2 red onions, finely chopped
handful of chopped parsley leaves
350 g (12 oz) tomatoes, chopped
125 ml (4¼ fl oz/generous ½ cup) olive oil
1 green (bell) pepper, chopped
1 red (bell) pepper, chopped
2 corn cobs, halved
250 g (9 oz) new potatoes
1 tablespoon salt
½ teaspoon ground black pepper
1 kg (2 lb 4 oz) green beans

In a large saucepan, combine the water, onions, parsley, tomatoes and olive oil. Cover and bring to the boil, then allow to bubble away for 5 minutes.

Add the peppers and cook for a further 1 minute over a medium-high heat before dropping in the corn and potatoes. If the liquid in the pot doesn't cover the vegetables, add a little more water so that they're just covered. Season with the salt and pepper then simmer, covered, for a further 5 minutes.

After this time, add the green beans and if they're sticking out of the water, add another glass or two of water to ensure they're covered.

Bring everything to the boil, then reduce the heat to low and simmer for 45 minutes–1 hour until most of the water has evaporated.

YIAYIA SOFIA

Born Ikaria, 1948

'I love dancing. The rebetika, Tsiftetelia, Kalamatiana. To dance a good *rebetiko*, you have to have something inside you and be able to express that in the dance. It was a talent of mine, to go with the rhythm. From dancing I then taught myself to play string instruments. That was what I did with my husband, we played music at the *panigiria*. I haven't played since he died a few years ago.

Wine gives you the *kefi* (desire) to dance. One glass, two glasses, three… I'll drink them and things will come out. I'll put my tumbler of wine down and pick it up with my teeth while I'm dancing. Things like this only come in the moment, to the music. It's part of the life of the *panigiri* to play with the dance.

I grew up in poverty and we lived off the land eating things like this *magirio*. We were five siblings, along with a few goats and cows. I would wake up before sunrise and walk from Raches to Evdilos to get to school. I stopped going eventually because it was too far to walk. It wasn't until 1979 that they built a road up here and we finally had electricity. We didn't realise that we were in hard times then though, we didn't have televisions so we couldn't compare ourselves to anyone else. Ikaria was really isolated until a few years ago.

When I was young, our *panigiria* would be for around 30 people, our fellow neighbours in the village. Now they've become so popular that thousands attend each one. Somehow, our tiny village festivals have become famous all over Greece.'

YIAYIA ATHINA'S GREEK CHIPS WITH FRIED EGGS AND TOMATO SAUCE FROM CRETE

Born 1913, Crete

Dedication by Marianna Leivaditaki, head chef at London's Morito restaurant and author of the cookbook Aegean

Yiayia Athina was a gift. She had the softest skin, a perfectly welcoming round face, long, brown, curly hair that you almost never got to see and large working hands. I met her when she was already old, widowed, always in black, and always having time for everyone. I used to spend hours and hours in her small kitchen, sitting on a wicker chair simply listening to her talk.

She had a beautiful marble sink, two gas hobs (stovetop burners), a table, some shelves with plates and cups and wicker chairs. The kitchen was the only room in her house that did not have pictures of saints on the walls. I was only tiny, but I never wanted to leave. An incredible storyteller, she would mesmerise you with her words and the only thing you wanted was to find out more.

Her kitchen was at the back of her house, but it was actually the main entrance. She never used the intended main door of the house. You walked down a small alleyway and there was a little wooden door that took you straight to her garden. Her garden was small, too, but what a space. It was an oasis, and always so cool despite the heat of the day. She had beautiful roses, the ones you can smell from afar and flowers everywhere that she watered every afternoon, while talking to them.

She wore black, in mourning for her husband Antonis, and a half apron with large pockets that always seemed to have treats in them, along with a paring knife. Her food was simple and wholesome. She would use ripe tomatoes and herbs and celery and the house would smell like what you imagine calmness and devotion would smell like if they had a scent.

The first thing she asked you when you walked into her house was, 'Are you hungry?' The best thing she used to cook for me was chips (fries) with fried eggs and her special tomato sauce. I can still smell the potatoes being fried in extra virgin olive oil and the eggs puffing up in another pan with yet more oil. She would sprinkle thick sea salt that her sons brought to her over the yolks while they were frying and fluffing up in the hot oil.

The chips took the longest to cook as they were hand cut into thick wedges. When ready, she would put them on a plate with the perfectly fried eggs and the most aromatic tomato sauce you have ever tasted. That was it. That was the dish I remember the most and miss the most. That is the dish I try to cook for myself in the same way, by wearing an apron and peeling the potatoes on my lap with a small knife whilst telling my son my stories. It is these memories, these images, these smells, that are deeply rooted inside. These are the things that help create the blocks of who we are.

This recipe is extremely simple and there is nothing much to it. It is a celebration of good ingredients used at their best and also a story about my memories of my yiayia.

However, you can play a lot with this recipe by adding wine and cured anchovies to the tomato sauce to make it more powerful, by grating cheese or adding fresh curd on top of the eggs, or by lacing the potatoes with truffle and Parmesan. Feel free to make your version of this. Use it as an idea rather than a recipe.

Serves 4
Vegetarian

FOR THE CHIPS (FRIES)
600 g (1 lb 5 oz) floury potatoes,
    peeled and cut into thick wedges
    (about 6 per potato)
300–400 ml (10–13 fl oz/
    1¼–generous 1½ cups)
    good-quality olive oil
coarse sea salt

FOR THE TOMATO SAUCE
100 ml (3½ fl oz/scant ½ cup)
    extra virgin olive oil
1 garlic clove, thinly sliced
500 g (1 lb 2 oz) tomatoes,
    roughly chopped
coarse sea salt

FOR THE FRIED EGGS
100 ml (3½ fl oz/scant ½ cup)
    olive oil
4 eggs
coarse sea salt

Place the potato wedges for the chips in a bowl of salted cold water and set aside for 15–20 minutes.

Meanwhile, make the tomato sauce. Heat the oil in a saucepan over a medium-low heat and add the sliced garlic. When the garlic begins to turn golden, add the tomatoes and season with salt, then cook over a medium heat for 10–15 minutes. You want to be able to smell the sweetness of the tomatoes, but you don't want to reduce or overcook the sauce. It still needs to retain some freshness. When ready, remove from the heat and let it rest.

Heat the oil for the chips in a saucepan until hot but not smoking.

Wash the potatoes under cold running water and pat them dry using a kitchen towel, then season them generously with sea salt before gently placing them into the hot oil in a single layer. You may need to do two batches, but this is fine. (You can keep them hot in the oven if needed.) Fry, stirring for 10–15 minutes until golden.

Finally, fry the eggs. Heat the oil in a frying pan (skillet) over a medium heat and break the eggs into it. Sprinkle some sea salt over the yolks and, using a spoon, baste the yolks with the hot oil. Remove the eggs using a slotted spoon and eat with the chips and the fragrant tomato sauce.

YIAYIA ANTHOUSA'S KOUNOUPIDI GIAHNI (CAULIFLOWER AND STEAMED RICE) FROM MILOS

I had a tip-off from a chef in Milos that Yiayia Anthousa was the most knowledgeable cook on the island, so we meet at a petrol station set somewhere between craggy volcanic beaches and meadows lush with wildflowers and smatterings of almost psychedelic poppies. She's in a muddied red Smart car and waves emphatically out of the window for me to follow her.

Although I've been to Milos before, I've never seen it quite so green. Spring is my favourite season in Greece and Milos is no exception. I follow Anthousa's car through pink and yellow fields of bleating goats, then onto winding coastal paths that wrap themselves around the island, the tarmac turning to dirt road and bumpy gravel that the Smart car ahead of me seems to be seasoned in traversing.

Her centuries-old house is on a hill with a view of the Aegean and in the distance on a clear day like today, we can make out Crete. On stepping out of the car, she holds her arms out wide for an enormous yiayia embrace and introduces herself by announcing her surname first, then her first name. I'm then whipped into the house where Anthousa swiftly begins to chop up a cauliflower.

Giahni in Greek means to 'cook in steam'. You can find numerous *giahni* dishes across Greece but this one, says Anthousa, is one that the people of Milos are best known for. Sweetened with tomato and sautéed onions, this hearty cauliflower and rice dish is one to cuddle up with on the sofa on a drizzly day.

Serves 4
Vegan

1 cauliflower, including the leaves
150 ml (5 fl oz/scant ⅔ cup) extra
  virgin olive oil
1 tablespoon salt
2 spring onions (scallions),
  roughly chopped (including
  the green tops)
1 red onion, finely chopped
½ teaspoon ground black pepper
1 heaped tablespoon tomato
  purée (paste)
160 g (1 cup) basmati rice
1 litre (34 fl oz/4 cups) water
chopped dill, to serve

Remove the florets from the cauliflower (don't make them too small – you want quite chunky pieces in this dish) and chop the stalk up into chunks before placing florets, leaves and stalks in a bowl and rinsing well.

Bring 1.5 litres (50 fl oz/6 cups) water to the boil in a large saucepan and add the cauliflower along with the salt, then boil on a high heat for 5 minutes. Drain and set aside.

Heat the oil in a large frying pan (skillet) or wok with a lid over a medium heat and fry the spring onions and red onion for 3 minutes, then add the cauliflower, cover and cook for another 10–15 minutes.

Add the pepper, tomato purée, rice and water and continue to simmer over a medium heat for 10 minutes, then reduce the heat to low and simmer for a further 20 minutes.

Garnish with the dill.

YIAYIA ANTHOUSA

Born Milos, 1962

'Obviously I'm biased but really, nothing can compare with the ancient history of this island. In 1820, the Aphrodite of Milos (*Venus de Milo*) was found here, and I find the story quite incredible. There was a farmer just digging up bits of his land, trying to find old bits of rock to build a house, and he turned up this ancient treasure. That's what they did in those days, they used ancient remains to build with. All the churches have been built with the ancient marbles. Thankfully, Aphrodite was saved.

There are other things to love about Milos. Our wells and springs have sustained the island for time immemorial. Our yiayiades here grew their own produce, and this dish comes from a time when we absolutely couldn't afford to throw food away. We'd make this when there were many cauliflowers. I learned the recipe from the ladies in the village and from my own yiayia, also called Anthousa.

I love being a grandmother. It's an interesting time of life for me. A completely different experience to being someone's mother. You get all the joy and much less of the anxiety and responsibility.

The most difficult thing I've ever gone through is losing my son in a motorcycling accident. He was only 25. There's no getting over it. I don't want to get over it, but I do want to live. I wear black for him, and I'll never take it off. I still paint my nails, I still dance and I still laugh, but the black I wear for him.'

YIAYIA ANNA'S MAKAROUNES (HOMEMADE PASTA) FROM KARPATHOS

I meet Anna in a flurry of fabric. She's dressed in the traditional folk costume of her village of Olympos, with a head scarf and many skirts trailing behind her as she hurries me through a narrow street to her taverna. The village feels very much disconnected from the rest of the world. Olympos lies in the clouds that hover at the end of a mountain pass on Karpathos island, which is already quite tricky to get to.

Up here, at least an hour away from any other signs of life, the people of Olympos have held on tightly to their customs. Yiayiades like Anna wear their dress daily, as their grandmothers did before them. The same goes for traditional dishes, homemade *makarounes* being one of these. Topped with sweet, caramelised onions and a generous grating of local cheese, this hearty pasta dish is one to see you through the winter.

Serves 5
Vegetarian

400 g (14 oz/scant 3¼ cups) plain (all-purpose) or 00 flour, plus extra for dusting
240 ml (8¼ oz/scant 1 cup) water
50 ml (1¾ fl oz/3 tablespoons) olive oil
2 large white onions, finely diced
grated Parmesan or graviera, to serve

Tip the flour into a large bowl and make a well in the middle. Pour a little bit of the water into it and, using your fingers, stir it in with the flour at the edges of the well. Add a little more water and continue to mix in the flour, adding more water until the mixture has come together.

Knead the dough for about 5 minutes, or until it has become smooth, pliable and elastic (you should feel it firm up as you knead). If it's too dry, add a tiny touch more water and, if it's sticky add a touch more flour. If you have time, leave the dough to rest in the bowl for 30 minutes, covered with a damp kitchen towel.

Flour the work surface lightly (too much flour will dry the pasta out), then pull a handful of dough from the bowl to begin shaping. Roll the dough into a long, thin rope about 1 cm (½ inch) in diameter. Cut the rope into 2.5–3 cm (1–1¼ inch) long pieces.

Now you need to make the *makarounes* shape: hold two fingers (the index and the middle finger) over the piece of dough, roll it ever so slightly away from you and then quickly pull it back while pressing firmly onto the dough, creating a curl and an indentation. Repeat until you've used all the dough, storing your shaped *makarounes* on a separate cutting board or tray.

Next caramelise the onions for your topping. Heat the olive oil in a frying pan (skillet) over a medium-high heat and fry the onions for up to 10 minutes, stirring often, until they take on a nice golden hue.

Bring a large saucepan of water to the boil and add plenty of salt (you want it to be salty like the sea). Cook the pasta for 2–3 minutes, then drain and serve topped with the onions and a generous grating of Parmesan.

YIAYIA ANNA

Born 1955, Karpathos

'I once left the island to live in Baltimore in America. I was only 19 and I kept hearing "America, America" and so I was enthused and decided to go there for some time. I didn't wear my traditional dress for the few years I was in the USA, but I did miss it. It's part of our way of life here. Many years ago, all the villages in Greece had their own dress. Unfortunately the tradition has been lost in the rest of Greece. The young girls in our village have also stopped wearing the dress, but if you come up here at Easter and watch the procession of the Epitaph, the entire village wears the old folk costume.'

YIAYIA ANGELIKA'S SPICY LEEKS GIAHNI FROM CORFU

Born Corfu, 1925

Dedication by Spyros Agious, head chef at Olivar restaurant, Corfu

When Yiayia got married, she moved to Corfu town and became a *proteuousiana*, which basically means a lady of good means living in the 'capital'. I remember her always being well-groomed, and she always said that not wearing lipstick felt like not wearing underwear. She often spoke in songs and her cooking was full of aromas and always delicious. Being very religious, she fasted very often and so had many 'vegan' specialties in her repertoire. One of them was this dish, which is one of my favourites.

The depth of flavour of this dish and the texture of the leeks that melt in the mouth with sweetness has been imprinted in my mind since I was a boy. All this, with only a few ingredients. It may sound funny, but the image of her with the large leeks in relation to her petite frame made this vegetable look even bigger when I was a child.

Yiayia Angelika's leeks *giahni* is classic, traditional Corfu cuisine. She followed the seasons and her food was always consistent in taste and generally very good. What I realised and especially appreciated over time, especially now as a professional cook, is the slow cooking, when she sautéed the onion very slowly until perfectly caramelised. The food reaches another level of taste if you take your time.

My yiayia's gift to me was that I learned to find beauty in simplicity and in the quality of seasonal produce on my own island. I understood that the key ingredient is love and that food is made up of memories and a wonderful collage of experiences.

Serves 4
Vegan

55 ml (1¾ fl oz/3 tablespoons) extra
  virgin olive oil, plus extra to serve
3 celery stalks, finely chopped
1 white onion, finely chopped
1 teaspoon ground allspice
2 garlic cloves, finely chopped
1 tablespoon paprika
½ tablespoon cayenne pepper
2 tablespoons tomato purée (paste)
125 ml (4¼ fl oz/generous ½ cup)
  water, plus extra as needed
5 leeks, trimmed and cut into 8 cm
  (3¼ inch) pieces
salt and freshly ground black
  pepper

TO SERVE
bread
feta (optional)

Heat the oil in a wide saucepan over a medium heat and fry the celery, onion and allspice for a couple of minutes until soft, without letting the vegetables brown. When they haved softened, add the garlic, paprika and cayenne and fry briefly to release their aromas.

Add the tomato purée and stir to release its deep red colour, then add the water and stir so that the purée becomes a sauce. Season with salt and pepper, then place the leeks on top in a single layer.

Add enough water to just cover the leeks, then simmer, covered, over a low heat for about 1 hour, or until they are soft, with some sauce left in the pan. Keep an eye on the leeks as they cook and if the water evaporates before the leeks are nicely softened, add a splash more. If you're worried your leeks are sticking, don't use a spoon to move them because they might break up in the pan. Pick the pan up and gently shake it in a circular motion.

Check the seasoning, then serve drizzled with a little more oil, alongside some feta and good bread for mopping up the sauce.

YIAYIA KATERINA'S TSOUHTI (TRADITIONAL EGG-TOPPED PASTA) FROM MANI

Dedication by Katianna Velos, home cook and founder of Golden Groves olive oil

There is no dish quite like *tsouhti*. The first bite instantly conjures nostalgic memories of long-gone summer evenings, squeezed into Yiayia's kitchen on the Mani Peninsula of the Peloponnese. The dish is named after the sound the mizithra cheese makes when it comes into contact with the hot oil and butter mixture – *tsouzei* in Greek means 'to sting'. The hot oil and butter foam up and make searing noises as the mizithra turns crisp and golden, effectively being stung by the simple sauce.

The sparing nature of this recipe is a testament to the humble agrarian origins of many of the inhabitants of my region. It's a frugal yet substantial meal made with the staples of any Greek household: olive oil, freshly made mizithra and dried pasta. The richness of the extra virgin olive oil and butter is offset by the sharp saltiness of the mizithra, a sheep's milk cheese that tastes better than any Parmesan, in my opinion.

Serves 5
Vegetarian

500 g (1 lb 2 oz) fat pasta for *pastitsio* (I like Misko no.2 like Yiayia Katerina used to, but any bucatini will do)
125 g (4 oz) unsalted butter
120 ml (4 fl oz/½ cup) extra virgin olive oil, plus extra for frying the eggs
100 g (3½ oz) grated aged mizithra cheese (or you can use matured cotija, Parmesan or kefalotyri)
5 eggs
salt and freshly ground black pepper

Bring a large saucepan of generously salted water to the boil, add the pasta and cook as per the packet's instructions.

Meanwhile, add the butter to a large frying pan (skillet) over a medium heat and as it starts to melt, add the olive oil.

Once the butter begins to brown slightly, add the cheese to the pan. The butter will begin to foam and make a hissing, crackling sound – do not fret, this is to be expected.

Turn the heat down to medium-low and use a wooden spoon to move the cheese around the pan for 2–3 minutes. This will ensure that the mizithra browns nicely, imparting an almost nutty flavour to the burnt butter.

In a separate frying pan, fry the eggs in olive oil, ensuring that the yolk is still runny.

When the pasta is cooked, drain it and add it to the pan with the cheese. Stir to coat, then remove from the heat and divide between plates. Season with plenty of pepper, then place an egg on top of each plate.

YIAYIA MARGARITA'S SKORDOMAKARONA (GARLIC AND TOMATO BUCATINI) FROM SANTORINI

Dogs, cats, horses and chickens watch on as Margarita serves a punchy pasta in the garden of her secluded house on the southern coast of Santorini. *Skordomakarona* brings together bucatini pasta, tomatoes that taste like sunshine and salty capers in one plate – a Santorini signature best enjoyed when the sun is out. An entire bulb of garlic goes into this, and I wouldn't skimp on it. Serve with Margarita's salad for a taste of rural island life.

Serves 4–6
Vegan

100 ml (3½ fl oz/scant ½ cup) olive oil, plus extra to serve
1 bulb of garlic, cloves chopped
600 g (1 lb 5 oz) tomatoes, chopped (if you can, use 2 large beef tomatoes – the juiciest and most organic you can find)
2 heaped tablespoons tomato purée (paste)
½ teaspoon granulated sugar
½ teaspoon sea salt flakes
500 g (1 lb 2 oz) bucatini
freshly ground black pepper, to taste
capers, to taste
feta, to taste (optional)

Put a large saucepan of water on to boil without salting it – this dish comes together in no time.

Heat the oil in a frying pan (skillet) over a medium heat and fry the garlic for a minute or so, taking care not to burn it.

Next, add the chopped tomatoes and tomato purée and crush the tomatoes with the back of a fork so that they become one with the paste, garlic and olive oil.

Add a sprinkle of black pepper, followed by the sugar and salt, and simmer for 5 minutes.

Meanwhile, generously salt the pasta water and add the bucatini. Cook as per the packet's instructions, taking care to stir the pasta so that it doesn't stick.

Drain the pasta, then add it back into the saucepan, followed by the tomato sauce.

Serve topped with a sprinkling of capers, crumbled feta and an extra drizzle of olive oil.

YIAYIA MARGARITA

Born Santorini, 1953

'I have my grandmother's name, Margarita. She was widowed young but she kept all the land left to her by my grandfather and worked it all herself. In those days we would make our own pasta and I remember my yiayia's was delicious. It was from her that I learned to make this dish and I think it was a regular in her repertoire because it was cheap, filling and fast to pull together. It's also a great option when we're fasting and observing vegan days for the 40 days before Easter and Christmas.'

YIAYIA LIZA-INSPIRED CHEESE AND LEMON RAVIOLI WITH SAFFRON FROM KOZANI

Dedication by Alex Vasilatou, head chef and founder of Alex, the fresh pasta bar, Athens

My nana is the perfect combination of tradition and innovation in cooking. Having excelled in classic Greek recipes, like taramosalata, oven-baked pasta, tender meat casserole and fried fish, she loved to try new things, adding special ingredients to surprise her guests. She likes to follow the recipe, but at the same time, she never actually does because food just needs a little extra something during the process that cannot be measured.

My style of cooking evokes the 'homey' feeling that my yiayia taught me. I constantly give love through my cooking, and this is something I inherited from Nana Liza. She always trusted my choices and believed I could make it in the food world and her confidence in my cooking made me follow my instincts and open my own pasta restaurant.

This dish was the first pasta dish that I created from scratch, mixing unique flavours together. I dedicated it to my nana because she taught me not to be afraid of putting together ingredients that are not 'classic combinations'. The ravioli features Greek saffron called 'krokos Kozanis' and the cheesiness with the sharp touch of lemon are flavours that remind me of her.

Serves 4–6
Vegetarian

FOR THE SAFFRON PASTA
400 g (14 oz/scant 3¼ cups) good-
   quality 00 flour, plus extra for
   dusting
240 g (8½ oz) whole eggs (from
   about 5 eggs)
pinch of saffron

FOR THE FILLING
40 ml (1⅓ fl oz/generous
   2 tablespoons) extra virgin olive
   oil
200 g (7 oz) leeks, finely diced
200 g (7 oz) onion, finely diced
150 ml (5 fl oz/scant ⅔ cup) lemon
   juice
200 g (7 oz) katiki Domokou
   (Greek cream cheese) or ricotta
50 g (2 oz) Gouda, grated
50 g (2 oz) edam, grated
50 g (2 oz) mature Cheddar, grated
80 g (3 oz) Parmesan, grated
zest of ½ lemon
salt and freshly ground black
   pepper

TO SERVE
knob of unsalted butter
toasted breadcrumbs

First, make the pasta. In a large bowl, combine the flour with the eggs and saffron. Bring it together, then knead on a lightly floured surface for 5–7 minutes until smooth.

Wrap the dough in cling film (plastic wrap) and refrigerate for at least 30 minutes. This dough makes around 30 pieces of ravioli.

Next, make the filling. Heat the oil in a frying pan (skillet) over a medium heat and sauté the leeks and onion for 15 minutes, or until very soft. When they have started to slightly brown, add the lemon juice and cook until the liquid evaporates. Set aside and allow to cool.

In a bowl, combine the cheeses, then add the leek and onion mixture, lemon zest and season to taste with salt and pepper.

Halve the chilled dough and then use a rolling pin and a floured surface, or better still, a pasta maker, to roll each section of dough into two thin sheets.

Use a teaspoon to add a heaped spoonful of the filling to the top of one sheet, leaving enough of the dough sheet around the filling (about 3 cm/1¼ inches) to make up the edges of the ravioli. Continue spooning out the filling onto the first sheet of dough, then when you have a line of evenly spaced filling running the length of the dough, bring the second sheet of dough on top of the first and gently cup your hand around the filling, gently pushing out any air around it and smoothing the dough to seal. You might still have filling left at this point but that's fine. Use a pasta cutter to cut ravioli shapes around the filling and collect the excess dough, then roll it again and repeat this process until you've used up the filling. Store the ravioli you have made on a tray lined with baking parchment.

Keep the ravioli in the refrigerator until you're ready to cook them (ensure it's the same day!), with a damp kitchen towel over the pasta to stop it from drying out.

When you're ready to eat, bring a large saucepan of salted water to the boil and drop the ravioli in. Cook for 1 minute, then drain, reserving some of the pasta water. Add the ravioli back into the pan with the butter and a ladle of the pasta water. When the liquid evaporates, serve with freshly ground black pepper and toasted breadcrumbs.

YIAYIA ANASTASIA'S ARAKAS LADEROS (BRAISED PEAS) FROM CORFU

Corfu can't lay claim to this dish as it's enjoyed all over Greece, but Yiayia does makes it her own with a generous dose of pepper. Again, we like our spices on this island and Yiayia never goes easy on the spices.

Another in Yiayia's *ladera* repertoire, these *arakas* demand a good amount of oil. The flavour is enhanced with garlic and plenty of salt and pepper, but it's the oil that really makes it so enjoyable. I often try to go without bread, as my carb requirements are covered in this meal thanks to the potatoes, but the sign of a good meal, in Yiayia's opinion, is a completely clean plate. There's always such a silky red sauce left over for dipping, that I always cave and give in to Yiayia's demands to scoop up every last remnant.

As with many of my grandmother's staples, this one is easy to throw together and feels so wholesome that I can eat plate after plate without feeling greedy.

Serves 4
Vegan

2 large potatoes, peeled and
  chopped into 2 cm (¾ inch) thick
  rounds
1 red onion, finely chopped
2 garlic cloves, finely chopped
1 kg (2 lb 4 oz) peas (fresh or
  frozen is fine)
1 heaped tablespoon cracked
  black pepper
1 tablespoon coarse sea salt
180 ml (6 fl oz/¾ cup) olive oil
700 ml (24 fl oz/scant 3 cups) water
1 tablespoon tomato purée (paste)

TO SERVE
bread
olives
feta (optional)

Put all the ingredients except the tomato purée into a large saucepan and bring to the boil, then simmer, covered, for 10 minutes.

After this time, add the tomato purée and simmer, uncovered, for a further 15 minutes, or until the water has evaporated and left you with a nice, oily sauce.

Serve with bread, olives and feta.

YIAYIA MARO'S REVITHADA (CHICKPEA STEW) FROM SIFNOS

I'm told that in Sifnos, locals use the neutral determiner *to* for many of their names. Maro introduces herself as 'to Maro' (the Maro) which I love because it implies there's only one Maro. When I mention her to others here, they know instantly who she is, so her name is nicely befitting. She's known for buzzing around Sifnos on her moped and for making the best *revithada* on the island.

Revithada is a slow-baked chickpea (garbanzo) stew that locals like Maro traditionally cook in a clay pot, in a wood-fired oven. It's absolutely effortless to whip up and features only a couple of essential ingredients. What makes the *revithada* so special is the time that goes into cooking it. Maro stresses the importance of baking it over a low heat for a number of hours.

In Sifnos, this is not a dish you might throw together on a Wednesday night after work. It's a dish traditionally made for Sundays, the flavours of the onion, bay and olive oil suffusing into a wholesome and hearty dish that only needs a slice of mizithra or a piece of bread for absolute perfection.

Serves 4–6
Vegan

500 g (1 lb 2 oz/2¼ cups) dried chickpeas (garbanzos), soaked overnight
2 onions, roughly chopped
2 bay leaves
½ tsp dried rosemary
1 teaspoon sea salt flakes
pinch of ground black pepper
90 ml (3 fl oz/generous ⅓ cup) olive oil
lemon wedges, to serve

Preheat the oven to 200°C (425°F/gas 7).

Drain the soaked chickpeas of water and add them to a clay pot, cast-iron casserole dish (Dutch oven) or tagine, followed by all the remaining ingredients. Top up with water to just cover the chickpeas.

Turn down the oven to 170°C (375°F/gas 5) without the fan on and bake for 6 hours, removing the lid after 4 hours and leaving it off if the water hasn't been soaked up by the chickpeas. Once you remove the lid, keep an eye on the chickpeas and ensure they don't dry out. You can also use a slow cooker for this dish, which will cut the cooking time down to 4 hours if turned to a high heat.

Serve with a wedge of lemon.

YIAYIA MARO

Born Sifnos, 1960

'In Sifnos we take more care over the cooking of our chickpeas than our meat. I have lots of animals – pigs, goats, chickens, ducks, rabbits – but it's my *revithada* that I will make for a Sunday and that's the way it has always been on the island. We're an island of farmers and chickpeas (garbanzos) were something we had a lot of. We might only eat meat on Easter and Christmas, but we were raised on chickpeas.

Then of course Sifnos is also known for its ceramics. When I was growing up many of the men on the island were potters. That left the women to farm the land and the children at home to prepare the family's dinner. That's how I learned to cook *revithada* myself, from the age of seven. Even on a Sunday, our parents would leave the house by donkey to go out and do their jobs out on the land and the *revithada* was an easy and filling dish for the entire family.

It might be a simple dish to make but the secret is in how it's cooked. When we were younger and for many generations before mine, the *revithada* would be prepared the night before in a ceramic pot with the family name or nickname written on it to separate it from the others, because we'd all take our pot to the village bakery and the chickpeas would bake in the bread oven overnight.

Most Sifnians still make it in a wood-fired oven, but of course you can take the recipe and recreate it in a gas or an electric oven. I would always advise it's made in a ceramic pot though, that's one ingredient I would never omit.'

YIAYIA MARIA'S LAHANODOLMADES
(CABBAGE ROLLS) FROM THASSOS

Born Thassos, 1912

Dedication by Bella Karragiannidis, food writer

Lahanodolamdes are the Greek version of cabbage rolls. Rice and ground meat are flavoured with seasonal herbs, wrapped in softened cabbage leaves and gently braised until they are melt-in-your-mouth tender. Cabbage rolls are a simple food that are made in different cultures all throughout Europe and the Middle East. Our family recipe for Greek *lahanodolmades* comes from our Yiayia Maria, whose legacy permeates our life and existence every day.

After being forced to flee her home in Turkey following the systematic elimination of Christians from the Ottoman Empire, her family lost and completely dispersed, Maria was left completely alone in the world. She married Lazaro at 17 and bore him seven children. They were so poor that the children would try to sneak spoonfuls of soup from their neighbours' kitchens.

Maria's husband died young but by that point, she had heard from her mother Koula, who'd emigrated to America and had managed to reunite with her husband (Maria's father) Gregori. Koula had managed to find Maria through her relatives in Greece and would regularly send money back to Greece to help her daughter. Once she found out that Maria's husband had died, she began to search for a way to bring her to America. Hope came in the form of Demo, who didn't have a family of his own. He promised to marry Maria and she moved to America to be with him and reunite with her parents.

Over the years in America, Yiayia Maria became a lover of pink flowers, Juicy Fruit gums, Kentucky Fried Chicken (which she called *kontouko*), and the TV show *Perry Mason*. Her cooking was simple and unassuming, just like her. She was most well known for her *lahanodolmades*. She ate cabbage so often that her house pretty much always smelled like cooked cabbage.

Sharing Yiayia Maria's story and her recipe for *lahanodolmades* is deeply meaningful. Refugees of war and immigrants are still risking their lives for the hope of a new beginning. While there is no easy solution to the current crisis, the simplest action we can all take is to unconditionally love. *Agape* (from the Greek *agapi*) is the deepest expression of love; it is totally selfless, never expecting anything in return. In this profoundly troubled time, may we choose to empathise, to love our fellow man with no demands, and to simply serve one another with *Agape* in whatever ways we are able.

Serves 4–6

1 large (or 2 medium) Savoy
    cabbages
2 tablespoons olive oil
1 onion, grated
2 garlic cloves, very finely chopped
500 g (1 lb 2 oz) minced (ground)
    beef or lamb
100 g (3½ oz/scant ½ cup)
    arborio rice
40 g (1½ oz) dill, chopped, plus
    extra to serve
40 g (1½ oz) parsley leaves,
    chopped
2 spring onions (scallions),
    chopped
1 teaspoon salt
½ teaspoon ground black pepper
700 ml (24 fl oz/scant 3 cups)
    chicken stock

FOR THE AVGOLEMONO SAUCE
4 eggs
juice of 1 large lemon or 2 medium
    lemons (about 120 ml/4 fl oz/
    ½ cup)
pinch of salt

Bring a large saucepan of salted water to the boil. While you wait for the water to boil, remove the core from the cabbage.

Stick a fork into the centre of the cabbage (where the core used to be) and dunk the cabbage into the boiling water until the outer leaves start to become soft (this takes about 3 minutes).

Remove the leaves from cabbage as they become soft and continue this process until all the leaves have been softened. Don't discard any small or torn leaves, as you will use them later.

Remove the thick portion of the main rib from each cabbage leaf with a knife and cut any especially large leaves in half if necessary.

Heat the olive oil in a frying pan (skillet) over a medium heat and cook the grated onion and garlic for about 10 minutes, stirring often, until the onions soften and lightly caramelise.

Combine the meat, rice, herbs, spring onions, salt, pepper and the cooked onion and garlic in a bowl, and mix until well combined.

Preheat the oven to 180°C (400°F/gas 6).

Place a cabbage leaf on the work surface and add a generous tablespoon of filling near the bottom of the leaf. Fold the bottom end up over the filling, then fold the two sides of the leaf inward and then roll the leaf into a bundle, making sure not to roll too tight as the filling will expand while it cooks.

Line a large casserole dish (Dutch oven) with leftover cabbage leaves (this is where you can use up any small or torn leaves). This keeps the rolls on the bottom of the dish from over-browning.

Arrange the cabbage rolls in the dish, packing them in snugly so they can't move around while cooking, then top the rolls with more leftover cabbage leaves. Pour in the chicken stock, cover and bake in the oven for 1½ hours.

When the cabbage rolls are almost ready, make the sauce. In a heatproof bowl set over a small saucepan of simmering water (or use a double boiler), whisk together the eggs, lemon juice and salt. Whisk constantly until the sauce begins to thicken – it is done when the whisk begins to leave a trail. Remove from the heat.

To serve, spoon the *avgolemono* sauce over the cabbage rolls and garnish with chopped dill.

YIAYIA KATINA'S STRAPATSADA (VILLAGE EGGS WITH TOMATO) FROM THESSALY

Yiayia Katina is rare in Greek grandmother terms. I hope no one will mind me saying this, but she's actually very sweet, whereas usually, the matriarch of the family is stern, wry and a bit of a force to be reckoned with. She always has a smile on her face and didn't mind at all when I asked her to climb over a ditch into a potentially snake-infested field for a photo. My own yiayia would not have had any of it.

She lives in a village of only 35 residents, a short drive away from the epic landscapes and teetering monasteries of Meteora, in what I like to call 'Middle Greece' on account of its fantasy-feeling rolling hills and verdant valleys. In reality, the region is Thessaly, a place on the map that is less frequented by tourists and abundant in tractors, sheep, cattle and the occasional wild boar (one scuttled out of the bushes across the road ahead of me on the drive up here from Athens and I had the fright of my life).

Her home is flanked by four expansive fields. The garden is dotted with combine harvesters, bright green tomato vines and quite often, half the village. They all call her *theia* (aunt) and drop by unannounced for coffee at all hours of the day.

I ask her if she ever gets bored of having to speak with the same people, day in, day out. Her response is telling of her pragmatism, 'I'm used to it now and I like the company. Besides, there's always someone getting divorced or someone dying, so we have new things to talk about according to which turns life takes.'

Together we make a village classic, *avga strapatsada*, which Yiayia Katina says could be eaten at any time of the day, but I deem it to be the perfect brunch. I like to serve this Ionian style, with a sprinkling of spicy cayenne pepper or chilli flakes, but the ladies in Katina's garden looked horrified at the mere suggestion. They say there's nothing better than a fresh slice of crunchy bread dipped into it, along with a crumbling of feta sprinkled on top.

Serves 4
Vegetarian

100 ml (3½ fl oz/scant ½ cup) olive oil
660 g (1 lb) good-quality passata (sieved tomatoes)
½ red (bell) pepper, chopped
8 eggs, beaten with a pinch of salt
salt

Heat the oil in a wide frying pan (skillet) over a medium heat and stir in the passata. Wait for it to start bubbling before adding the chopped red pepper.

Add a sprinkling of salt and allow to bubble away for 10–15 minutes until the peppers are soft and the passata and oil have combined into a nice sauce.

Once the sauce has thickened, add the eggs and marble into the tomato with a spoon. Take care to stand over it and stir occasionally to make sure it doesn't stick and burn.

Cook for 10 minutes until the eggs are cooked but still soft (if you see the eggs hardening faster and it's becoming a little omelette-like, take it off the heat).

YIAYIA KATINA

Born Thessaly, 1935

'All of us *Karagounes* (women that traditionally wore the Karagouniki outfits in the 19th century) in the village make this food. My grandmother taught me how to make it. She practically raised me and was always at home to cook something or share what she knew in the kitchen. I still remember her now and the thought puts a smile on my face.

I started working out in the fields as a teenager. We'd start work at 6 a.m. and work the land because where we live, cotton and wheat are abundant and agriculture has always been the main industry. These eggs were a quick fix for when we'd come back from a tiring day out on the land. We have always had hens in the garden for fresh eggs and our tomatoes – even in winter – are some of the best in Greece.

They call this tomato "Italiki" because it's believed to be Italian in origin. This particular variant has been in my family for at least 100 years now, and we make a point of keeping seeds from the very best fruit from each harvest for the next year. All we do is dry them out in the sun, then plant them the following summer. When they're ripe, we remove the skins and bottle them. This way, we lock in flavour and have tomatoes to use all winter.'

Feasting

YIAYIA EVANGELIA'S BEEF PASTITSADA FROM CORFU

Pastitsada is my all-time favourite dish. It nods to my island's geographical proximity to Italy. You can see the very southern point of Puglia from Corfu's most north-western tip. It makes sense, then, that this dish has its roots in Italy. Originally known as *pastissada de caval* (on account of it being made with horse meat once upon a time) the dish was brought to Corfu by the Venetians in the 1400s.

I make it with Yiayia Evangelia, who's from the famous Lavranos family of butchers on the island. Very much on island time, she doesn't sweat that it's 11 p.m. before we have a chance to taste this incredible dish. She regales me with stories of the Corfu of olds and fills me with ripe figs. She waves me off with a bucket full of waxy aubergines (eggplants) and bulbous tomatoes to take home to my own yiayia.

Corfiots like to overcook their pasta, but I'd advise eating the bucatini al dente and topping this off with a great big slab of feta. It's the ultimate show-off dish. Serve with a simple tomato and cucumber salad

Serves 6–8

1.5 kg (3 lb 5 oz) short ribs, washed
100 ml (3½ fl oz/scant ½ cup) extra virgin olive oil
300 g (10½ oz) red onions (about 2 onions), finely chopped
7 garlic cloves, chopped
½ tablespoon sea salt flakes
2 tablespoons tomato purée (paste)
200 ml (7 fl oz/scant 1 cup) red wine
3 large beef tomatoes, grated into a bowl
1½ teaspoons ground cinnamon
1 heaped teaspoon ground cloves
1 heaped teaspoon ground black pepper
2 bay leaves
1 heaped teaspoon paprika
½ teaspoon cayenne pepper
500 g (1 lb 2 oz) bucatini

Put the washed short ribs into a large saucepan and heat over a low heat to allow the water to steam off the meat. Turn the meat if you can see it beginning to brown on one side. Once the water has mostly evaporated, add the olive oil. Increase the heat to medium and brown the short ribs, turning them occasionally to ensure they don't stick on one side.

After a minute or so, while they are still browning, stir in the onions and garlic, then scatter in the salt.

When the meat is a nice deep brown, add the tomato purée and stir well. Cook for a further 5 minutes, then pour in the red wine and cook for 5 minutes more to allow the alcohol to cook off.

Add the grated tomatoes and their juices and stir in, turning up the heat a little. The sauce should be a nice orangey red colour. Now add all the spices, stir and cover the pan. Reduce the heat to low and simmer away for 2 hours. Stir it occasionally, ensuring the meat isn't sticking to the pan and is covered by the sauce.

After 2 hours, remove the lid and allow any excess water water to cook off before putting your pasta on to boil. You should have a very rich, rust-red looking sauce and at this stage, the meat should almost be falling off the bone.

Bring a large saucepan of generously salted water to the boil and cook the bucatini as per the packet's instructions.

Drain the pasta, then add it back into the saucepan, ladling some of your rich red sauce into the pan and tossing it with the pasta. Yiayia Evangelia serves her short ribs separately on a platter, allowing everyone at the table to fight over their piece of meat.

YIAYIA EVANGELIA

Born Corfu, 1941

'Many young men wanted me, but when I met my husband it only took one look and that was it. He came to see me at my sister's house, accompanied by my uncle, and I liked him from the very beginning. His eyes caught my attention. Then he went off to the army, but when he came back we would sometimes meet in secret in the olive groves. All around this house there was absolutely nothing at all but fields and olive groves when I was that age. I had three brothers who were very protective, so we had to meet covertly.

In marriage it's important to have balance. The man sometimes wants it his way but no, that's not the way we do it in my house. I have as much of a say in things as he does. He'll try to get involved with my cooking because he's a cook as well, but I like to do things my way. This dish I like to make with short ribs because it makes the *sugo* tastier.

I liked working at the butchers when I was younger. I think it was the chatting to customers that I enjoyed the most. Around the holidays there was always such a buzz at the shop. For example on 15 August for our celebration of the Assumption of Mary, it's traditional in Corfu to eat this *pastitsada*. Everyone would come in to the shop in the lead up to the day to buy the best cut of meat.

The shop's still in the family now and they're doing really well with it. We still employ the old techniques, using the entire animal and making sure that nothing goes to waste. I love the *noumboulo*, our smoked pork cold cut from Corfu.'

YIAYIA KOULA'S KOTOPOULO LEMONATO (LEMON ROAST CHICKEN) FROM ANDROS

Born Peloponnese, 1930

Dedication by Melina Giolva, co-founder of Zymi baked snacks

Yiayia Koula is the strongest female figure I've ever known, co-existing with her in this life is one of my biggest blessings. Until her last breath she never stopped impressing me with her determination, fierce attitude, inner peace and unconditional love.

Her main love language was preparing food for her family. She was from the Peloponnese, but love brought her to the island of Andros in her late twenties. I spent my first summer with her when I was only a month old. I remember her using her retro cooking utensils from the 1970s, which she would insist were irreplaceable on account of their quality.

During the summers I never had an alarm, it was the smell of what she was cooking in the mornings that would always wake me up and bring me straight to the small traditional kitchen she had. She taught me how to forage, harvest and prepare my own capers, how to cultivate vegetables and how to make sure every year we have enough chickens for our own eggs. She was obsessed with her lemon tree, which she planted when I was born. I knew that one of my daily tasks would be to collect the eggs in the morning and cut a few lemons for her that she would then use for our meals, like this *kotopoulo lemonato*. After her passing I've probably never eaten or will ever eat food that has been prepared with so much love.

Serves 4

6 large potatoes, peeled, halved
  lengthways, then cut into thirds
1 chicken, jointed
3–4 large garlic cloves, sliced
50 ml (1¾ fl oz/3 tablespoons) extra
  virgin olive oil
1 heaped tablespoon dried oregano
2 vegetable stock cubes dissolved in
  650 ml (22 fl oz/2¾ cups) water
juice of 2 lemons
1 heaped tablespoon mustard
salt and freshly ground black
  pepper

TO SERVE
salad
feta

Preheat the oven to 170°C (375°F/gas 5).

Scatter the potatoes in a large roasting tin. Arrange the chicken pieces between the potatoes and make a couple of 2 cm (¾ inch) deep incisions in each piece of chicken by stabbing into it with a small, sharp knife. Slide the sliced garlic into these incisions.

Drizzle the olive oil over the chicken, then sprinkle with the oregano and a pinch each of salt and pepper (you won't need a lot as the stock is salty enough).

Pour over the vegetable stock (it shouldn't entirely cover the potatoes but should come up to two thirds of their height in the tray) and lemon juice. Rub the mustard into the portions of chicken that still sit above the water.

Roast in the oven for 1½ hours. If the chicken starts to get a little too dark on one side, turn it over and add a splash of water if it needs to cook for longer.

Serve with a leaf salad and hefty chunks of feta. You can use the chicken bones to make a broth for *gamopilafo* (see page 158).

YIAYIA MARIA'S KOLOKASSI KAI XOIRINO (TARO AND PORK STEW) FROM CYPRUS

Born 1907, Cyprus

Dedication by Maria Elia, chef, consultant and author of the cookbook Smashing Plates

Following the Greek tradition, I was christened with my yiayia's name. My Yiayia Maria lived in Gerakis, a small village in the Troodos Mountains of Cyprus, where she raised five children. My dad would walk the goats they kept around the mountain every morning before school while my yiayia tended the land they owned where they grew fruit and vegetables. She would make wine and *zivania* (pomace brandy) from their grapes and *soutzouko*, a popular sweet (candy) made from grape must and almonds. Up until the age of 80 she would ride her donkey side saddle around the village.

When I was around four, she came over to London to help my father run his restaurant. She was one of the most hard-working people I have ever met and I wish I'd got to spend more time with her. Once a week we'd visit Shepherd's Bush Market, her favourite place to shop since they stocked so many fresh Cypriot ingredients it made her feel like she was at home, and I treasured our times together there.

This recipe fills me with nostalgia and is one she would make once a week. Kolokassi is a root vegetable also known as taro. In Cyprus it's cooked in a tomato-flavoured pork or chicken stew delicately flavoured with celery. If you want to make this with chicken, replace the pork with bone-in thighs and legs. It's also just as delicious made without the meat if you're vegetarian.

Serves 4–6

1 kg (2 lb 4 oz) kolokassi (taro)
4 tablespoons olive oil
1 kg (2 lb 4 oz) pork (I like mine on the bone so I use pork loin chops, but you can use diced shoulder or neck)
1 large onion, chopped
6 large celery stalks, strings removed and thickly sliced
2 tomatoes, peeled and roughly chopped
4 tablespoons tomato purée (paste) dissolved in 250 ml (8½ fl oz/ 1 cup) water
juice of ½ lemon
chopped parsley leaves
salt and freshly ground black pepper
crusty bread, to serve

To prepare the kolokassi, cut off the ends and peel the skin, then wipe clean with a wet cloth – never wash kolokassi with running water. Using a sharp knife, chip or crack away irregular pieces, about 3 cm (1¼ inches) in size. If you slice the kolokassi all the way through it releases a sticky juice and will turn to mush while it's cooking.

Heat half the oil in a deep saucepan over a medium heat. Season the meat with salt and pepper, add to the pan and brown on all sides. Remove and set aside.

Heat the remaining oil and gently fry the onion until soft, then add the kolokassi and celery. Fry for 5–10 minutes, or until they start to colour.

Place the tomatoes and meat on top of the vegetables. Pour over the tomato water, season with a little salt and pepper, then bring to the boil, cover and simmer gently for 1 hour, or until the pork and kolokassi are both tender.

Add the lemon juice to taste and parsley, and serve with lots of crusty bread (Greek knotted sesame bread if you can!) to mop up the juices.

YIAYIA DESPINA'S GAMOPILAFO (WEDDING RISOTTO) FROM CRETE

Despina lives just outside of the Venetian fortress of Chania in Crete. Her garden is in bloom when I arrive, thick with orange blossom and hefty lemons hanging off branches like precious jewels. We actually harvest lemons straight from Despina's tree for this iconic Cretan dish, but before getting started, she insists that I try the yoghurt cake she's made for me (an entire tray) and a couple of nutmeg biscuits with a silty Greek coffee.

She's been recommended to me by a friend who had the pleasure of being cooked for by Kyria Despina when he was at university many moons ago, so I've been pre-warned of her hefty portion sizes.

The soul-feeding *gamopilafo* is a creamy rice dish made from goat, rooster or chicken broth and is traditionally served at weddings here in Chania, and all over Crete. It literally means 'wedding rice' and is a nod to the city's Venetian past, a long-lost cousin of the risotto.

It's always made for people in large numbers so Despina cooks up enough to feed a family of ten and proceeds to serve me three helpings. I've trimmed down the quantities and recommend using roast chicken broth. It's a handy way to put your roast chicken leftovers to good use, though you can also use vegetable stock if you want to make this vegetarian. If you're wanting to cook up a feast, I'd pair it with a lemon roast chicken.

Serves 4–6

1.5 litres (50 fl oz/6 cups) chicken stock
70 g (2½ oz) unsalted butter
1 tablespoon salt
500 g (1 lb 2 oz/2¾ cups) Karolina rice (arborio rice also works well if you can't get hold of Karolina), washed
juice of 2 lemons
leftover chicken or Greek yoghurt, to serve

In a large saucepan, bring the chicken stock to the boil and add the butter and salt.

Add the rice to the stock, reduce the heat to medium-low and stir constantly until the rice has soaked up the liquid and is a risotto consistency. This should take 20–25 minutes.

Remove from the heat and add the lemon juice.

Eat immediately with any chicken leftovers stripped from the bones of the chicken or add a good blob of Greek yoghurt on the pilaf once served.

YIAYIA DESPINA

Born Chania, 1946

'In Chania we always eat this at weddings. Rice has for a very long time been symbolic at Greek weddings. We throw rice as the bride and groom take their first steps as man and wife, following the priest around the church wearing the joined *stefania* (crowns) that bind them in their new life together. Rice at weddings goes back to before Christianity though, the ancient Greeks also featured it in their ceremonies. We've always liked a good wedding here. We Cretans have good humour. If there's an excuse for a dance, we'll use it.'

YIAYIA ELEUTERIA'S ROAST LEG OF LAMB WITH ORANGES AND POTATOES FROM CRETE

We're making this dish in advance of Orthodox Easter, sand between our toes on Crete's southern coastline. I've never had a roast lamb with oranges before and love the idea of bringing these ingredients together. After 40 days of fasting, lamb is the star of any Greek Easter spread and I prefer a leg roasted in the oven with soft, citrus-infused potatoes to meat on the grill any day. To master this dish is to be able to provide the ultimate Greek family feast forever, so I'm particularly excited that Yiayia Eleuteria is sharing her taverna's famous recipe.

Eleuteria knocks this together and has it in the oven within ten minutes of us meeting. She deftly chops potatoes directly into an oven tray, and I watch her, completely dazed at how fast she moves. It seems wrong to ask a woman that is so clearly in command of her kitchen if she'd like any help.

Of course, it comes out perfect: brown, caramelised and crisp on the outside, tender and melting in the middle. The potatoes benefit from the extra liquid that the orange juice brings to the dish and that final hint of citrus makes the entire tray of lamb all the more succulent. The recipe goes down well at Easter lunch when I test it. Serve this with Eleuteria's Dakos (see page 94).

Serves 4–6

330 ml (11¼ fl oz/1⅓ cups) extra virgin olive oil
juice of 4 oranges, plus 1 orange, sliced, for garnishing
2 tablespoons honey
2 tablespoons Dijon mustard
2–3 kg (4 lb 8 oz–6 lb 9 oz) leg of lamb
7 large garlic cloves
½ teaspoon coarse sea salt
6 large potatoes, peeled and quartered
1 tablespoon dried oregano
3 bay leaves
240 ml (8¼ fl oz/scant 1 cup) water
sea salt flakes

Preheat the oven to 200°C (425°F/gas 7).

In a jug (pitcher), mix together the olive oil, orange juice, honey and mustard.

Place the lamb in a large roasting tin and make four deep incisions in the meat with a small, sharp knife. Fill each incision with a clove of garlic and the coarse sea salt. Pour half the oil and orange juice mixture onto the lamb, then place the potatoes around the leg before pouring the rest of the orange mixture over it everything.

Sprinkle over the oregano and add the bay leaves, followed by a scattering of sea salt flakes.

Crush the remaining garlic cloves over the potatoes, then pour in the water.

Cover the tray with foil and roast in the oven for 1 hour. After this time, check how the lamb is progressing and remove the foil so that it browns. Return to the oven and cook for a further 1 hour, checking it every 15 minutes or so by slicing into the thicker part of the leg and checking the colour on the inside. Top up with a little more water if needed. Yiayia Eleuteria likes hers cooked to medium, but if you prefer rare and want your lamb to still retain a little pink in the middle, keep an eye on it. If you're roasting a smaller leg, the total cooking time will be less – it may only need 30 minutes after taking the foil off.

YIAYIA ELEUTERIA

Born Tertsa, 1957

'We've had our taverna for 20 years. We're lucky enough to be in an agricultural area where all of Crete's produce grows. Whatever Greece is eating, Crete is growing and it's growing here in the south where I'm from. The area's famous for feeding the entire country. That's not the only special thing about Crete. I love my island because we're known for being the most welcoming here. It's in our nature to open our doors to strangers. The concept of *filoxenia* must have started in Crete. I'm sure of it.'

KYRIA GOULA'S KARAVIDES YIOUVETSI (CRAWFISH ORZO) FROM TRIKERI

Goula lives in the village of Trikeri, about an hour's drive from the port town of Volos, through the lush, mountainous region of Pelion. Just below her village is the Pagasetic Gulf, which feels more like a lake than it does the sea. Boats bob gently on the water and I'm bizarrely reminded of the Lake District in the north of England, only with bright blue skies and sunshine.

We walk past abandoned, crumbling homes to get to Goula, who has refused to move from the village in the hills down to the coastline where most of the other inhabitants have gone. I enter Kyria Goula's through a beaded curtain, into a wood-clad room that boasts a 'secret' pantry, a wooden door inconspicuously cut into the varnished wood of the walls. It's in here that she has around 10 kilos of pasta stored, 'just in case'. There's no running water in her home and she still uses an outhouse toilet. We cook on a gas burner that Goula positions on the floor just in front of the door to her kitchen, and I'm amazed at what a feast can come from the most humble kitchen.

Being by the sea, Goula shows me how to make the region's crawfish *yiouvetsi*, a satisfying pasta dish that tastes of a Greek summer. Kyria Goula swears by using the juiciest tomatoes and only when they're in season.

Serves 6

100 ml (3½ fl oz/scant ½ cup) extra virgin olive oil
2 large onions, finely chopped
2 large beef tomatoes
1.2 litres (40 fl oz/4¾ cups) water
1 tablespoon coarse sea salt
½ teaspoon black peppercorns
1 kg (2 lb 4 oz) crawfish (you can also use langoustines)
500 g (1 lb 2 oz) orzo
handful of parsley, chopped

Heat the olive oil in a large saucepan over a medium-high heat and fry the onions. Let them sizzle a moment while you grate the tomatoes; the skin should be left in your hand at the end – don't use this in the dish. Add the grated tomato to the pan, stir, then cook for 5 minutes.

Add 200 ml (7 fl oz/scant 1 cup) of the water, the salt and pepper, then reduce the heat to medium and cook for a further 10 minutes.

Add the crawfish, followed by the remaining water. You want the water to just about cover the crawfish. After 8 minutes, remove the crawfish with a slotted spoon and set aside before stirring the orzo into the pan. Cook for a further 15 minutes with the lid off until the orzo is al dente. Stir often so that the pasta absorbs the stock like a risotto and doesn't stick to the bottom of the pan. Pop the crawfish back into the pan for 2 minutes with the lid on before the end of the cooking time to reheat. Transfer to a serving dish and garnish with fresh parsley.

KYRIA GOULA

Born Agia Kyriaki, Magnessia, 1944

'We always had such an excess of crawfish in the village that we have a lot of recipes featuring them. I first made this recipe when I was eight years old. My brothers would go out in the *kaikia* (traditional fishing boats) for fish and in the nets they'd also pull up crawfish. They'd sell the fish and bring the crawfish home for us to eat. That's how this dish originated in the region. We would also make our own homemade pasta once upon a time, but orzo does just fine.

My own father was out fishing when I was just a baby and never came back. At the time, there was an epidemic of people fishing with dynamite. It was obviously much easier than going out and laying nets, but more destructive and dangerous. I was five months old when I lost my father in this way. People just didn't know any better in those days.

My brothers thankfully helped a lot when I was a little girl. They would walk all the way down the mountainside to collect water because we had no running water in the village until the late 1960s. It was a simple existence and we were poor but I didn't mind at all, I had everything I needed. I still don't have a tap in the house, I collect rainwater and use the tap outside.'

NONNA THALIA'S SCORPION FISH BOURDETO (SPICY FISH STEW) FROM CORFU

Born 1923, Corfu

Dedication by Apostolos Porsanidis-Kavvadias, olive oil producer and founder of Dr Kavvadia

Nonna Thalia came from a well-educated family. She lived in Corfu Town until the Second World War and then she moved to Athens, where she met a young prominent doctor, Apostolos Kavvadias, whom she married.

Thalia was a strict woman of impeccable taste. If times had been different, she might have been an architect, but she did well raising three daughters and managing Dr Kavvadias' fortune. She convinced him to buy an old abandoned olive press next to a dirt road on central Corfu and insisted on renovating the space into a home. In the year 1950 it was the very first olive press in Corfu that had been transformed into a house, and later on the dirt road that led to it would become the main road connecting Corfu Town to the north of Corfu. My family and I inherited the most amazing space thanks to her persistence (and my pappou's hard work).

Studying design, I realised how creative Nonna was. She used simple found objects to decorate her home, always somehow making them look chic and expensive. Her bedhead was an old metal door frame, her dishes were made in a small artisanal pottery. She always used beautiful local ceramics to serve the food on, some of which we still use.

The family lived in Athens so our Corfu home was mainly used as a vacation house when I was little. I remember the journey would be so long and we'd always arrive late at night, but my grandparents would be waiting for us and on arrival, the entire house was filled with the aromas of Nonna's scorpion fish *bourdeto*.

Nonna Thalia knew that less is more and followed this rule when she cooked. All her recipes were based on amazing produce, cooked beautifully. That is the essence of Greek food, Greek nature and Greek life.

Today our home and farm on Corfu is alive again. We raise our family here and produce olive oil. Behind all of this is my yiayia. She made me love this place, and offered me and my family the opportunity to live a different life here at the farm. My designs are based on her take on life. Less is more. The simple things make for the most complex creations. Form follows function...

I miss her a lot. I miss her wisdom and life lessons and her assurance that everything will be alright. She is behind every stone at Dr Kavvadia's organic farm.

Serves 6

2 kg (4 lb 8 oz) scorpion fish, gutted
1 heaped tablespoon sea salt flakes
100 ml (3½ fl oz/scant ½ cup) extra
  virgin olive oil
2 large onions, finely chopped
2 teaspoons sweet paprika
2 teaspoons spicy paprika or
  cayenne pepper
1 litre (34 fl oz/4 cups) vegetable
  stock
juice of 2 lemons

Rub the fish with the salt and let them sit for at least 20 minutes.

Heat the oil in a wide, shallow pan over a medium heat and sauté the onions until they are softened and light golden brown. Mix in the two paprikas, stir to combine and cook for a further minute or so.

Add the fish to the pan, followed by the stock. Bring to the boil, then reduce the heat and simmer for a further 30 minutes, or until the sauce has thickened. Remove from the heat and add the lemon juice before serving.

Note: Apostolos insists there's no potato in a Corfiot **bourdeto** *but I have seen many a yiayia drop a potato or two in there, likely for more sustenance. If you like the idea of bulking this up, simply add peeled and chopped potatoes when you add the fish.*

YIAYIA TOULA'S BIANCO
(WHITE FISH WITH POTATOES) FROM CORFU

I've been admiring Toula's handiwork for years before I manage to pin her down and finally cook her famous *bianco* with her. Her eponymous restaurant in Agni Bay towards the pebble-strewn north-west coast of the island plays host to visiting yachts and their often famous owners in the summer months. Toula has cooked for Kate Moss, she's hosted a birthday party for Prince Harry ('The boys and their friends were all very lively that night') and counts the Rothschilds as regulars. The bianco (meaning 'white') is a simple white fish dish with plenty of flavour. Corfiots like to proudly explain that the dish's name is not Greek but Italian, nodding to the island's proximity to Italy and to its links with the conquering Venetians. Originally a poor man's lunch, owing to the fact that fish, lemons and olive oil were abundant around the island, the dish is one every Corfiot yiayia knows well, including my own. Toula adds a touch of innovation, throwing in a couple of cardamom pods for their lemony aroma. Yiayia Toula serves this with a crisp glass of Assyrtiko wine and crusty bread.

Serves 4

1 kg (2 lb 4 oz) white grouper, sliced into steaks (you can also use an alternative silver fish like sea bream or sea bass – if using one of these, ensure it's been gutted and add it in whole)
2 tablespoons salt
120 ml (4 fl oz/½ cup) olive oil
1 kg (2 lb 4 oz) new potatoes, peeled and chopped
1 tablespoon dried oregano
½ teaspoon cracked black pepper
4 cardamom pods
3 large garlic cloves, roughly chopped
2 lemons

Prepare the fish by rubbing the salt into the flesh and allowing to sit for 30 minutes.

Drizzle 2 tablespoons of the olive oil into a wide saucepan and add the potatoes. Sprinkle over the oregano, pepper, cardamom, garlic and the zest from ¼ lemon. Place the fish on top of the potatoes and top with another 2 tablespoons of olive oil.

Pour in water so that it reaches the middle of the pan. It should just cover the potatoes and the bottom of the fish but not drown it entirely. Cover and bring to the boil, then whip the lid off once it's bubbling, reduce the heat to medium and allow to cook for 10 minutes. Try not to move the fish too much and don't stir the contents of the pan.

After 10 minutes, carefully turn the fish over. The aim is to not stir at all, as the fish can fall apart easily at this point. Simply lift the fish off the top with a slatted spatula or spoon and turn it over.

Cook for a further 10–20 minutes, depending on the fish you have chosen. If you're cooking a white grouper and have bought a thick steak from the fishmonger, it will likely need a little longer, whereas sea bass and bream will need less.

Remove the pan from the heat – it should still have some liquid in it, which you'll want for dipping.

Mix together the juice from both of the lemons with the remaining olive oil, then pour this on top of the fish, followed by the zest from one of the lemons. Check the seasoning and adjust as needed.

YIAYIA TOULA

Born Corfu, 1955

'I wasn't always destined for the restaurant life. I was such a keen student that as a girl, I dreamed of becoming a doctor and going to Africa to work there. I started reading aged four. I always had my head in a book and I was inspired by a book I was reading. Even now with the restaurant, I still read a lot. A lot of what I've learned about food has come from books.

The plan was to leave the island to go and study in Athens but in the end, I fell in love. What could I do? My husband-to-be was an electrician and in those days it wasn't the done thing here in Greece for a woman to have a more esteemed profession than her husband. Thankfully, things are no longer like that, but it was the case for me.

I don't mind that this is how life worked out, though. I love Corfu. The smell of fresh earth when it rains here (which it does a lot, in the winter). The smiles of my neighbours and the people in my village. I love this spot, where my restaurant is. Looking out over the water here, I feel safe. It feels like a hug. Albania is so close we can see it from here and the sea feels more like a lake because of that. We see dolphins here in the winter. Its beauty never fails to make me appreciate my life. It's the appreciation of what we have, not the mourning of what we've lost, that makes a person truly happy.'

YIAYIA LILY'S XTAPODOMAKARONADA (OCTOPUS PASTA) FROM CORFU

Lily isn't your typical yiayia in that she isn't Greek, but she can knock up a better spicy *makaronada* than most of the yiayiades on the island. That's because she's married to Kyrios Bellos, owner of my favourite establishment in Corfu, Klimataria, and an arbiter of taste when it comes to traditional Corfiot dishes like this one. At their restaurant, Kyrios Bellos keeps a watchful eye over customers, always prepared to ask 'What was wrong with it?' if a plate returns to the kitchen with even a scrap of food on it. Meanwhile, Lily can be found in the kitchen, stirring a hot saucepan or else hastily plating up desserts, all of her own making.

Like my own mother, Lily found herself in Corfu on account of falling for a Greek man. She arrived on the island from Ireland during a golden period of tourism here, watching the village of Benitses transform from quaint fishing village to a party hot-spot in the 1980s.

This octopus pasta is both a signature of the island and of Klimataria. I'm in awe of the fact that I now hold the key to making perhaps one of my favourite dishes in the way that it is served at my most frequented Corfiot eatery. The octopus cooks in a rich sauce of olive oil, spicy pepper and tomato and is served with spaghetti. Both the pasta and the addition of spices nod to the Italian influence on Corfu, the conquering Venetians bringing spice to the island from their expeditions further east.

Lily insists on beating the octopus before it's cooked. In fact, she adds hers to a cement mixer bought especially for this task. Lacking a cement mixer of my own, I tend to buy a frozen octopus, then thaw it slowly before cooking, which also tenderises the octopus nicely.

Serves 4–6

1.6 kg (3 lb 8 oz) frozen octopus, defrosted
3 large red onions, roughly chopped
250 ml (8½ fl oz/1 cup) olive oil
½ teaspoon cracked black pepper
½ teaspoon hot paprika or cayenne pepper
1 litre (34 fl oz/4 cups) warm water
2 tablespoons tomato purée (paste)
500–700 g (1 lb 2 oz–1 lb 10 oz) spaghetti (Lily's favourite is Barilla no.3)

Rinse the defrosted octopus and massage it as you do. Lily likes to massage hers for 20 minutes, even after it's been in the cement mixer.

Chop the head off, slicing 2 cm (¾ inch) rings from the head, then cut the tentacles into 7 cm (2¾ inch) chunks before placing it into a wide and shallow casserole dish (Dutch oven).

Place the dish over a high heat and allow the water to cook off for 30 minutes with the lid on – you'll see a lot of water comes off the octopus.

Meanwhile, blitz the onions in a food processor. You can finely chop the onions if you don't have a food processor but blending them is better as it will give you a silkier sauce.

Continued overleaf >

After 30 minutes of the octopus steaming in its own water, add the olive oil and onions. Stir everything well so that the octopus doesn't stick.

Stir in the pepper and paprika, then cover the octopus with the warm water. Cook over a high heat for about 40 minutes until the octopus is tender – you want to be able to stick a toothpick in it and pull it out again. Throughout the cooking time, check the octopus isn't sticking and stir frequently, and supplement with an extra glass of water if it needs it.

Towards the end of the cooking time, stir in the tomato purée. If the sauce is looking a bit dry, add a little more water – the octopus can only get more tender the longer it cooks.

When the octopus is tender, remove from the heat and leave a lid on it while you cook the spaghetti. Bring a large saucepan of salted water to the boil and cook the spaghetti until al dente, as per the packet's instructions. Serve with the octopus and sauce.

LILY

Born Ireland, 1953

'Once, my mother and father visited from Ireland and I asked them to try this dish. I said to my dad, 'You really must try this, it's Greek sausage.' (They loved sausages and potatoes.) So he ate it and it seemed to go down very well. Then when I told him at the end it was an octopus that he'd eaten he proclaimed it had made him feel sick.

Greece was almost an exotic place to the Irish back in the 1970s when I first arrived in Corfu. I'd met my husband working in a travel agency back home and we moved over here together. When my mum and dad first met him, they didn't know what to expect – that's how used to foreigners they were.

When we first moved to Corfu there were very few of the amenities I'd been used to back in Ireland. There were no streetlights, so at night I'd have to go out with a torch. My mother-in-law's was the first house in the village to have a television. I remember everyone would just pile into the house and gather outside the window to watch TV. There was rarely a moment of quiet or peace, always people coming in and out and I had to get used to the home not necessarily being a private space. A good lesson I've picked up in life is to tolerate everything that comes your way and learn to cope with it.'

YIAYIA NIKI'S BAKALIAROS PLAKI (COD BAKE) FROM KALAMATA

Deep into the mountains, up winding passes and a rough, rugged terrain between which olive trees and drooping eucalyptus burst forth, Niki is the only inhabitant of her village on the rugged Mani Peninsula. She lives in a stone house, with centuries-old embroidery framed and hanging from the walls, along with traditional wooden instruments, religious icons and sepia photographs, faded even more by the sun.

Niki is a healer. She says she's never been to a doctor in her life and swears by the power of raw vegetables and fruit. She is a rare breed here in Greece, less obsessed with feeding me an overwhelming amount of food and more concerned about making sure she gives me the right thing to truly nourish. Seconds into our meeting, she's passing me a beetroot, carrot and apple juice she's made. Then Marco the pony makes an entrance, helping himself to the basket of apples on the floor. Petting him and calling him 'Markaki', Niki doesn't seem to mind one bit and I feel like I've walked into a scene from a 1990s children's TV show.

We eat Niki's flavour-rich dish in the dappled shade of her balcony, overlooking inky blue water in the distance. The currants perfectly balance the salted cod, but if you're not a fan of salt cod, I've also made this recipe with cod fillets and added salt myself. I've also made this into a plentiful vegan dish by omitting the fish and adding an extra potato and red (bell) pepper.

Serves 4–6

1 kg (2 lb 4 oz) salt cod or cod fillets
120 ml (4 fl oz/½ cup) olive oil
2 onions, roughly chopped
3 large garlic cloves, roughly chopped
600 g (1 lb 5 oz) potatoes, roughly chopped
4 bay leaves
1 cinnamon stick
½ teaspoon peppercorns
5 cloves
5 allspice berries
100 g (3½ oz/⅔ cup) currants (Zante currants)
1 red (bell) pepper, roughly chopped
130 ml (4½ fl oz/generous ½ cup) water
500 g (1 lb 2 oz) tomatoes (can be tinned), quartered
bunch of parsley, chopped (including the stalks)
dried oregano, to taste
sea salt flakes
bread, to serve

If using salt cod, soak the fillets overnight in water, then the next day, rinse again under cold water, drain and squeeze the fillets to remove any excess water.

Lay the fish flat in a baking dish and sprinkle with oregano, then set aside.

Preheat the oven to 180°C (400°F/gas 6).

Heat the oil in a large non-stick frying pan (skillet) with a lid over a high heat and fry the onions, garlic and potatoes for 5 minutes.

Add the bay leaves, spices, currants and red pepper, along with a final sprinkling of oregano and 80 ml (2¾ fl oz/⅓ cup) of the water. Cover and steam for 10 minutes, stirring occasionally so that the potatoes don't stick. If you're using cod that hasn't been salted, sprinkle in a tablespoon of sea salt flakes at this point.

Add the tomatoes and cook for a further 2 minutes with the lid on, then remove from the heat and pour the mixture over the cod in the baking dish.

Sprinkle half the chopped parsley over the top and the remaining water, then bake in the oven for 40 minutes.

When cooked, garnish with the remaining chopped parsley and serve with a slice of bread for soaking up the juices.

YIAYIA NIKI

Born Kalamata, 1939

'Inside, I feel like I'm 15 years old, despite having lived so many lives in one. I was born in Kalamata and I had seven children with an Englishman, from the age of 20 until 34. My mother and grandmother always said, "Have however many children God wants to give you," so I did. I honestly gave birth to them like nothing was happening to me. Just one pain and out.

I raised them all on raw fruit and vegetables. Cooking produce destroys vitamins, so where I can, I eat salads and juices. This dish is traditional from the area, but I like to reserve the parsley to add in last for this purpose. It's something I'll eat on a Sunday because it's fish. I never eat meat. My children were raised practically vegan and I remember friends and family thinking I was completely mad but none of them has ever seen a doctor.

The people from the Peloponnese are wild and unfriendly, somehow. I'm not sure how my family and I became such open people. I've become a grandmother to far more children than I ever expected to. The monks in Mount Athos had heard about the family and they began to send lost children our way, young people who were drug addicts and needed to detox. I would take them in and help them.

By that point I had divorced my first husband because he was far too strict with the children. I wanted my children to be free and to make their own decisions in life and his way was too restrictive. My son left here when he was 14 and went to live with Bedouin in the Egyptian desert. I think children should be allowed to make their own choices and be given freedom to grow into who they are. Somehow, mine all found their way and have become successful, autonomous and creative people with their own talents and interests. They amaze me.'

Treating

YIAYIA MARIA'S 'GREEK' COFFEE

I spot Yiayia Maria sweeping up outside her son's restaurant on Kastellorizo's harbour on a hot May morning. She's tiny and very frail but absolutely will not accept any help when I offer it. Neither will she let me go to the bakery for her (she's on her way there after doing the morning clean up).

Old she may be, but Yiayia Maria is known across the whole island as the keeper of Kastellorizo's secrets. She knows the entire history of the island and is the last survivor of a major catastrophe that occurred when a ship bringing back Greek refugees after the war sank on its way to Kastellorizo from Egypt.

Despite the notorious Greek–Turkish tensions that have developed since the great population exchange of 1918, Yiayia Maria surprises me with the warmth she shows towards her neighbours on the Turkish mainland, just a mile away from Kastellorizo. She slowly brews me a rich Greek coffee and indulges me with her stories, as well as the ultimate recipe for our most loved morning pick-me-up.

As well as finely ground Greek coffee, you'll need a copper briki pot with a long handle to make one of these.

Some essential rules from Yiayia Maria:

Always, always, always brew the coffee over an open flame.

If you're just making a *mono* (a single coffee for one), use a smaller briki. If you're making a *diplo* (a double) or coffee for two, you'll need a larger size.

Don't stir the coffee while it's on the heat because this stops it frothing and ultimately the froth, or *kaymaki*, is what lends the coffee its distinct, rich flavour.

Serves 1
Vegan

1 heaped teaspoon Greek coffee
sugar, to taste (optional)

Combine the Greek coffee and sugar, if using, in a briki. In Greece, levels of sweetness range from *metrios* (medium; 1 teaspoon of sugar for every teaspoon of coffee) to *glykos* (sweet; 2 teaspoons of sugar for every teaspoon of coffee). If you're making coffee for more than one person in a larger briki, add an extra teaspoon of coffee per extra person.

Measure out the water with the espresso cup you'll be using to drink your coffee and pour that into the briki.

Stir just enough to ensure the coffee grounds and sugar are combined with the water. Never stir while the coffee is on the heat.

Place the briki on a small gas ring and allow it to come to the boil slowly over a low flame. Keep watch over it and as it begins to rise and froth, remove from the heat. Yiayia Maria then brings her coffee up to a froth one final time before taking it off the heat and serving.

Pour the coffee into a small cup, including the sediment, which is a chief characteristic of this coffee.

YIAYIA MARIA

Born Kastellorizo, 1931

'What's the difference between a Greek coffee and a Turkish one? Nothing. It's all the same. It's a bit like people. Some call themselves Greek, others say they're Turkish, but in the end, there aren't any differences at all. Before there was "Greece" and "Turkey", we all used to live alongside each other. We have the mosque here in Kastellorizo and when my mother was a girl, a whole section of our population was Muslim. Then after the First World War things began to change and before I was born, most of the Muslims living among us had left to go over to the Turkish mainland.

We Kastellorizans never had problems with our neighbours across the water. It was the Germans that bombed us and the Second World War that made refugees of us. We were forced to abandon Kastellorizo when its population had reached 15,000 residents. Now there's less than 500 of us left. It was too dangerous for us to live here during the Second World War so we fled east, to Palestine, where we lived for four years in tents.

I remember I was just a little girl when we were able to come back, but it wasn't a joyous occasion. The ship that we came back on left Egypt but within a day, it had caught fire and we lost my youngest sibling in the evacuation attempt. My mother married at 13 years old and had 16 children. This was her last baby and they drowned on the way back to Kastellorizo. We were rescued just in time to see the ship break in half from the flames and sink. Then we had to sit in the Suez Canal for a week, waiting for another ship to finally bring us to our little island.

Even after the war, we kept good relations with those opposite us on the Turkish mainland. We would go shopping for groceries over there every Friday and if anyone was ever in need of a good doctor, it was to Turkey that they would go. They were always welcomed with open arms. It is politics that gets in the way of human friendships. My own husband was sent to prison for taking coffee over to Turkey when it wasn't allowed. For centuries, trade had passed between us but suddenly, there were laws restricting that, and my husband was sent to prison for four years.

They've parked a warship on our little harbour and the army's fighter jets fly over every now and then, but when there's a wedding, we're all invited over to enjoy the festivities with our Turkish friends. They also come over for Easter. When my husband died, they brought 17 wreaths over to lay on his grave. Greek or Turkish, it's the same blood that runs through all our veins.'

YIAYIA KONSTANTIA'S KOLOKITHOPITA STRIFTI (SWEET PUMPKIN PIE) FROM HALKIDIKI

In Thessaloniki, I become so obsessed with filo rolling that I make it my mission to find yiayiades in the region to show me how it's done. Originating in Eastern Anatolia, Pontic Greeks like Yiayia Konstantia are credited for bringing pies to Greece. Not stodgy or meaty, these pies are made of delicate, crispy filo wrapped around wild greens, pumpkin or a crumbling of sharp, salty cheese.

I drop by Konstantia's for a demonstration in her village home in Halkidiki, a 40-minute drive through lush countryside from Thessaloniki. She handles the rolling pin so deftly and moves it so fast across the table that I worry it might fly away from her and hit me in the face, hypnotised by the repetitive motion that turns a ball of dough into an ultra-fine sheet of pastry. I have a go and find I'm absolutely useless in comparison, resolving to practice or forever resign myself to ready-made pastry.

'My entire village moved from Turkey to Halkidiki. Most of our cuisine comes from the Polis,' Konstantia tells me, referring to Constantinople (the name Greeks nostalgically use for Istanbul).

This sweet pumpkin pie is made with a very standard recipe for filo. What makes Konstantia's distinct is her expertise in rolling the homemade dough so fine. If you're not quite as skilled as she is in this department or pressed for time, you can always use ready-made filo sheets. The filling of sweet pumpkin, sultanas (golden raisins), cinnamon and crunchy walnuts also happens to make this regional sweet treat particularly special.

Serves 20
Vegan

2 kg (4 lb 8 oz) pumpkin or squash, peeled, seeds scooped out and chopped into chunks
1 tablespoon semolina
100 g (3½ oz/scant ½ cup) granulated sugar
100 g (3½ oz/generous ¾ cup) chopped walnuts
1 heaped teaspoon ground cinnamon
50 g (2 oz/scant ½ cup) sultanas (golden raisins)
pinch of salt
light olive oil, for greasing
500 g (1 lb 2 oz) filo pastry (see page 39, or use ready-made filo pastry sheets)

FOR THE SYRUP
1 lemon
500 g (1 lb 2 oz) sugar

Preheat the oven to 180°C (350°F/gas 4).

Place the pumpkin in a large roasting tin lined with baking parchment, cover with kitchen foil and bake in the oven for 45 minutes, or until very soft.

Once cooked, remove from the oven and leave to cool in a couple of sieves placed over large bowls, then break up the pumpkin with a fork or masher, mashing into it so that any extra moisture can escape and you're left with a nice pumpkin mash. Keep the pumpkin water and set aside, to make the syrup with later.

Add the cooled pumpkin to a large bowl and combine with the semolina, sugar, walnuts, cinnamon, sultanas and salt.

To assemble the pie, prepare a 35 cm (13¾ inch) round baking tray (pan) or a couple of pie tins or round casserole dishes (anything with a solid bottom to hold the syrup) by coating the insides with a drizzle or two of light olive oil.

Open up a sheet of filo on your work surface and brush it lightly with olive oil. Spoon about 3 tablespoons of the pumpkin mixture across the bottom of the filo sheet in a line, leaving around 2.5 cm (1 inch) of space at the bottom to be able to fold over.

Fold the bottom over the mix and continue rolling so that you create a sausage. Don't roll this too tightly or you may find it hard to bend your sausages into the spiral pattern we're creating next.

Place this sausage in the very middle of the baking tray, bending it round on itself to create the start of a spiral. Repeat the last step again and as you add each filo sausage to the tray, follow on from the one before, creating one long spiral that runs from the inside of the tray all the way to the edge. The spiral should be tight with no gaps.

If you have made your own filo, follow Yiayia Konstantia's lead and slice the pie into eight large pieces before it goes into the oven so that once it's out, it soaks up the syrup nicely.

Daub the top of the pie with a brush or two of light olive oil, then bake in the oven for 45 minutes, or until it is deep golden and crisp.

Meanwhile, make the syrup. Measure out 500 ml (17 fl oz/2 cups) of the pumpkin water – if you don't have enough, top it up with water. In a saucepan, combine this with the sugar, the zest of the whole lemon and juice of half, then bring to the boil. Reduce the heat and simmer for 15 minutes. Pour the syrup over the pie as soon as it's out of the oven. Leave to cool before serving.

YIAYIA KONSTANTIA

Born Halkidiki, 1937

'Now that you can buy ready-made filo, I do wonder who's going to set out troubling themselves rolling their own homemade dough. Women nowadays work and have less time to commit to time-consuming things like this at home. It's a shame, because these skills we've fostered for generations, even since before our families came to live in Greece, will be lost. You have to really want to do this well and do it right to commit to doing it from scratch. It's become second nature for me, but it's not an easy skill to learn, rolling filo sheets this thin. You have to practice a lot to get to do it as fast as I do.

My entire village was called Plagia and it was just outside of Constantinople. Then in the population exchange of 1922 when all the ethnic Greeks had to leave Turkey, pretty much the entire village picked up and left, coming here to Halkidiki. That's why the village is called Nea Plagia, meaning "new Plagia."'

YIAYIA NOTA'S GREEK NEW YEAR AND EASTER TREATS

Born 1924, Arcadia

Dedication by Ianthi Michalaki, head baker and founder of Kora Bakery, Athens

Together with her brother and father, Yiayia Nota fled from Arcadia to Athens during the war, where she found work in a clothing factory. That's where she met my pappou. He was a manager at the factory and Yiayia would proudly tell us how jealous all her friends were when he picked her. I remember them being happy together despite their very different personalities. Yiayia was a firm and dynamic woman who ran a tight ship around the home. Sometimes, I think how great she'd be at running a professional kitchen. Out of all my family, she was the only one who got excited when I dropped out of medical school to become a chef. We've always shared a passion for cooking and a love for good food and I believe it made her very happy that someone in the family would finally carry on in her footsteps.

Growing up with a mother who thought boiled potatoes made for a sufficient lunch, Yiayia's visits were a bright light in my milk-and-cereal filled life. We would all spend summers together in Agios Stefanos in Corfu, where I have some of my most precious memories of Yiayia. A table full of all the best meze – *skordalia*, courgette (zucchini) fritters, chips (fries), tomato salad and roasted aubergines (eggplants) – waited for us after a day at the beach. *Loukoumades* and *tiganopsomo* (fried dough often filled with cheese) in the afternoons, when all the children played in our garden. There isn't a single person in my family who doesn't have nostalgia for Yiayia's cooking.

Yiayia passed away the year I went to culinary school. She would ask me curiously over the phone for tips and recipes and tried to write it down so she could give it a go. After years of training and experience, I still can't make her *portokalopita* (orange pie) and *melomakarona* (honey biscuits/cookies) as well as she did. I take great comfort and joy knowing how happy she'd be to see the bakery I have set up and how I've managed to build a career around food, the thing she loved so much.

Around the holidays I always get emotional making her *tsourekia* or *Vasilopita*. This year, I used her *Vasilopita* recipe at the bakery. Yiayia's cooking shaped my perception of food and it's through her that I connect with all the culinary traditions of my country.

I know everyone has a great Yiayia, but mine was truly the best.

YIAYIA NOTA'S VASILOPITA (NEW YEAR CAKE)

Serves 12
Vegetarian

90 g (3¼ oz) unsalted butter, at
   room temperature
250 g (9 oz/1 cup plus 4 teaspoons)
   caster (superfine) sugar
220 g (7¾ oz) whole eggs (from
   about 4–5 medium eggs)
40 ml (1⅓ fl oz/generous
   2 tablespoons) milk
40 ml (1⅓ fl oz/generous
   2 tablespoons) water
175 g (6 oz/scant 1½ cups) self-
   raising (self-rising) flour
¼ teaspoon baking powder
1 teaspoons ground cinnamon
½ teaspoon ground nutmeg
pinch of salt
zest of 1 orange
70 g (2½ oz) yoghurt
50 g (2 oz/½ cup) walnuts, chopped

Preheat the oven to 160°C (350°F/gas 4) and grease and line a
23 cm (9 inch) cake tin (pan).

In a large bowl, beat together the butter and sugar until pale
and fluffy.

Gradually add the eggs, a little at a time, mixing well after each
addition. Once all the eggs have been incorporated, beat for
a further 2 minutes. Add the milk and water and mix again for
1 minute, scraping down the sides of the bowl.

In a small bowl, combine the flour, baking powder, cinnamon,
nutmeg and salt. Add the dry ingredients to the egg mixture and
mix until well incorporated.

In another bowl, mix together the orange zest and yoghurt. Using
a rubber spatula, fold it into the cake batter until smooth. Finally,
fold in the chopped walnuts.

Pour the mixture into the prepared cake tin and bake in the oven
for 45–50 minutes. Once baked, hide a lucky coin inside.

YIAYIA NOTA'S TSOUREKI (EASTER BREAD)

Serves 8
Vegetarian

80 g (3 oz) fresh yeast
120 ml (4 fl oz/½ cup) lukewarm
  water
1 kg (2 lb 4 oz/8 cups) strong
  white bread flour
200 g (7 oz) whole eggs (from
  4 medium eggs), plus 1 egg yolk
  for the egg wash
170 ml (5¾ fl oz/scant ¾ cup) milk,
  plus extra for the egg wash
100 g (3½ oz) unsalted butter,
  melted
270 g (9½ oz/scant 1¼ cups) caster
  (superfine) sugar
30 ml (2 tablespoons) orange juice
zest of 1 orange
1 teaspoon ground mahleb
1 teaspoon ground cardamom
1 teaspoon ground mastic
flaked (slivered) almonds, to finish

Preheat the oven to 160°C (350°F/gas 4) and line a baking sheet with baking parchment.

In a small bowl, combine the yeast, water and 150 g (5 oz/scant 1¼ cup) of the flour. Mix well, cover with a kitchen towel and leave somewhere warm for 1 hour until it doubles in volume.

In a large bowl, combine the yeasted pre-mix with the rest of the ingredients and knead well for 15–20 minutes (it's painful but essential – you must knead until it feels like your arms might fall off). Once you have a smooth, elastic dough, cover again with a kitchen towel and leave somewhere warm for 2 hours. Make sure to use a bowl much larger, as the dough will rise significantly during this time.

Portion the dough in two or three pieces and shape them like baguettes. Let them rest on the work surface, covered, for 15–20 minutes. This will help you work the dough better in the following steps.

Start working the dough outwards, pushing the air out and creating longer and thinner strands. Braid them together, then place the *tsoureki* on the prepared baking sheet. Cover again with a kitchen towel and leave to rise for 1 hour at room temperature.

Once proved, lightly beat the egg yolk with a little milk and brush it all over the *tsoureki*. Dust with flaked almonds and bake for 40–45 minutes.

YIAYIA THEIOCLEIA'S LOUKOUMADES (DOUGHNUT BALLS) FROM CRETE

There are four generations of women on hand to rustle up a mountain of *loukoumades* at Yiayia Theiocleia's house. Her daughter, granddaughters and great granddaughter welcome me with the kind of warmth I'd expect from my own family. All smiles and tight squeezes – the Cretan way, it seems.

We quickly get to making up an assembly line with Yiayia Theiocleia at the head, sat in a chair, rifling through a recipe book she's been adding to for the past 70 years, followed by me, her daughter and granddaughters, all on hand to sift, mix, whisk and fry at her every command.

Essentially doughnuts but much more elegant, *loukoumades* are theorised to be a very Greek dessert. Yiayia Theiocleia makes a point of telling me they were served at the first Olympic Games thousands of years ago, but variations of these sweet doughnut balls can be found in Persian and Turkish kitchens too.

We eat them with a drizzle of honey, cinnamon and sesame seeds, but a blob of vanilla ice cream wouldn't go amiss here – especially if you're serving them warm (the very best way to enjoy them).

Serves 6–8
Vegetarian

8 g (1 tablespoon) active dry yeast
520 ml (17 fl oz/generous 2 cups)
  lukewarm water
1 heaped teaspoon salt
500 g (1 lb 2 oz/4 cups) plain
  (all-purpose) flour
700 ml (24 fl oz/scant 3 cups)
  sunflower oil

TO SERVE
honey
ground cinnamon
sesame seeds

In a bowl or small jug (pitcher), combine the yeast with half the water and leave in a warm place for about 5 minutes, allowing the yeast to react.

In a separate bowl, combine the salt with the remaining water and set aside.

Sift the flour into a large bowl, create a well in the middle and pour in the water and yeast mixture bit by bit, mixing as Yiayia Theiocleia does, by hand.

Once the yeast and water mixture has been added, pour in the salted water, again adding it bit by bit as you continue to mix by hand. As you mix, squeeze the very loose dough mixture in your palm and lift it into the air, allowing the yeast to do its magic. Keep doing this and stirring until the mixture is smooth. If you're still encountering lumps, work with a large whisk to smooth them out. You want the mixture to be very light and silky, which might require an extended whisking period. It's worth it in the end.

Once you're happy with the dough's consistency, leave it somewhere warm, covered with a kitchen towel, for 30–40 minutes until it has triple in size.

When it has risen and you can spot a few small bubbles in the dough, you can get going with the frying.

Heat the oil in a dry, deep frying pan (skillet) or wok over a high heat. Drop a tiny piece of dough in there to check if the oil is hot enough – you want it to sizzle immediately on contact.

Time to work fast. For perfect, round *loukoumades*, work with your hand and a tablespoon, dropping your hand into the dough mixture and lifting some out, making a fist with your hand so that some of the dough slips neatly through the space between your thumb and forefinger. Swiftly scoop this with your tablespoon and drop it in the frying oil. (It helps to have a mug of water next to the bowl so you can dip the spoon in and clean it before adding each new dough ball.)

Allow the dough ball to fry for 30 seconds or so, then use a slotted spoon to turn it over. It should be nicely browned all over. Fry in batches, but be sure not to overcrowd the pan because the *loukoumades* will stick together. Transfer the loukoumades to paper towels to drain.

Serve with a drizzle of honey and a sprinkling of cinnamon and sesame seeds.

YIAYIA THEIOCLEIA

Born Crete, 1931

'I used to make so many batches of these *loukoumades* along with hundreds of other sweet things when my kids were young. *Kalitsounia* (sweet cheese pastries), *tiganites* (pancakes), *loukoumades* – they're all versions of pastry with honey but well-loved among us Cretans.

We celebrate saints' days here in Greece and instead of hosting a party for a birthday, we'll celebrate the day of the saint we were named after. I remember back in those days when anyone was hosting a name day party, we'd leave our porch light on outside or use a gas lantern if we didn't have electricity and that would be the signal for everyone in the neighbourhood to come over for the party. It was an open house for anyone who wanted to join.

I'd spend the entire week before any of these parties preparing *dolmades* and other savoury dishes but it's the sweet treats like this one the women in the neighbourhood really went in for. The house would be packed full of people but I loved it. I've always been the hostess.

Then, of course, because so many people came over to my name day parties, I had to get my daughter to write down the names of the families attending, so I could make sure we wouldn't miss their name day when that date in the calendar rolled around. Otherwise, they'd take offense!'

YIAYIA ASIMINA'S PISTACHIO
SPIRAL BAKLAVA FROM AEGINA

Born 1929, Piraeus

Dedication by Mina Stone, cookbook writer and chef at Mina's NYC

By the time I was born, my Yiayia Asimina (my namesake) and three of her sisters were spending their summers in Aegina, an island famous for its brilliant green pistachios. As my grandmother got older, she started living there full time and my fondest memories are of grocery shopping with her.

When I would visit, I would always rent a car, usually a rickety one, and she would tease me and say, 'Finally, my chauffeur has arrived.' We would drive to the main town together and go to all the special markets. The butcher to get rabbits, the fish market for anchovies, the laiki for fruit and vegetables.

Our final stop would always be the bakery. I could never resist tearing into the warm bread the second we got home and spreading butter and honey on multiple pieces while Yiayia looked at me out of the corner of her eye, worrying I'd spoil my appetite.

In the afternoon, she loved making baklava, and had her own special shape for it that I have never seen anywhere else – a spiral, bite-size round, topped with crushed nuts. She would make baklava with walnuts and almonds, but after spending years in Aegina she would decorate them with crushed pistachios.

This baklava recipe uses only pistachios. It is a nod to Aegina and also a nod to her Pontic heritage, as pistachios are often used for desserts in and around Asia Minor. My great-grandmother fled from Georgia during the population exchange of 1923 and my yiayia would reminisce about her often, teaching me words in Pontic Greek.

Makes 40–50 pieces
Vegetarian

30 g (1 oz/2 heaped tablespoons)
   granulated sugar
2 teaspoons ground cinnamon
½ teaspoon ground cloves
600 g (1 lb 5 oz/4 cups) raw
   pistachios, shelled
350 g (12 oz) salted butter,
   plus extra for greasing
500 g (1 lb 2 oz) ready-made
   filo pastry

FOR THE HONEY SYRUP

350 g (12 oz/1 cup) honey
   (preferably Greek thyme honey)
500 ml (17 fl oz/2 cups) water
2 cinnamon sticks
1 tablespoon lemon juice

Preheat the oven to 180°C (400°F/gas 6) and grease a 23 x 28 cm (9 x 11 inch) baking sheet.

In a bowl, combine the sugar with the cinnamon and cloves.

In a food processor, pulse the pistachios until they resemble coarse breadcrumbs.

Mix three quarters of the pistachio crumbs with the sugar mixture and set the rest aside for garnish.

Melt the butter in a saucepan over a low heat and then skim off the white froth and milk solids that rise to the surface of the melted butter. This is now clarified butter. Set aside.

Unroll the filo and place one sheet in front of you, oriented vertically. Brush with the clarified butter using a pastry brush or your hands. Place another sheet of filo on top and butter it, repeating to create a stack of 4 layers of buttered filo.

Spread about 100 g (3½ oz) of the sugar and pistachio mixture evenly over the filo stack, then roll the nut-covered filo into a log from top to bottom. Cut the log into about eight pieces, around 4 cm (1½) inches wide.

Place the pieces, spiral side up, on the prepared baking sheet, leaving just a little bit of space between each piece of baklava.

Repeat with the remaining filo and spoon any remaining nut mixture over the tops of the baklava. Brush the tops generously with butter and bake in the oven for about 40 minutes until golden brown.

Prepare the honey syrup while the baklava bakes. Combine the honey, water and cinnamon sticks in a saucepan and bring to the boil.

Reduce the heat and simmer until the syrup is slightly thickened, 7–10 minutes. Remove from heat and add the lemon juice, then let the syrup cool to room temperature.

Pour the syrup over the hot baklava when it comes out of the oven. The baklava will sizzle a bit as you pour the syrup over it. When the baklava has cooled, sprinkle the tops with the reserved pistachios.

YIAYIA ANGELIKI'S KOULOURAKIA (SPICED BISCUITS) FROM ATHENS

There's nothing more *yiayiadistiko* (in the style of a Greek yiayia) than a tray of freshly baked *koulourakia*. My own yiayia dips these in her coffee every morning and has a never-ending supply in her cupboard. They're especially handy come Sarakosti, the fasting periods in the Greek Orthodox calendar in which we adopt a vegan diet.

Yiayia Angeliki is an expert at crafting the perfect *koulouraki*. The spices are perfectly balanced with a citrus kick from the oranges, meaning less sugar is required to make them really tasty. Together we knock up a batch of three trays, Angeliki beating me in a *koulouraki* shaping race many times over.

Dip these biscuits into a Greek coffee or serve as an accompaniment to an iced freddo cappuccino.

Makes 30 biscuits
Vegan

80 g (3 oz/⅓cup) caster (superfine) sugar
4 large oranges
2 teaspoons ground cinnamon
½ teaspoon ground cloves
pinch of salt
65 g (2½ oz) vegan block butter or margarine, softened
1 teaspoon bicarbonate of soda (baking soda)
1½ teaspoons baking powder
50 ml (1¾ fl oz/3 tablespoons) cognac
100 ml (3½ fl oz/scant ½ cup) neutral-tasting oil (Angeliki uses corn oil but you can also use sunflower or plain sesame oil)
600 g (1 lb 5 oz/generous 4¾ cups) plain (all-purpose) flour, plus extra for dusting

Preheat the oven to 180°C (400°F/gas 6) and line two large baking sheets with baking parchment.

In a large bowl, combine the sugar, the zest from the 4 oranges, the cinnamon, cloves and salt. Beat in the vegan butter with a wooden spoon until pale and fluffy.

Juice 2 of the oranges into a jug (pitcher), passing it through a sieve to catch the bits. Stir in the bicarbonate of soda, baking powder and cognac and pour it into the bowl with the sugar and orange zest. Stir to combine.

Follow with the oil, then mix in the flour a little at a time until the mixture comes together as a dough. Work the flour in with your hands, kneading a little bit – the dough should be smooth and ever so slightly wet, but not sticky. Add a touch more orange juice if you feel it's too dry, or a touch more flour if too wet.

Now make your *koulourakia* shapes: take a walnut-size piece of dough (around 35 g/1¼ oz) and roll it between your palms into a ball. Then, on a lightly floured surface, roll it into a sausage shape, and keep rolling until it is about 1 cm (½ inch) in diameter.

Bend the sausage into a U shape, twisting both ends of the 'U' over and around each other so that it incorporates two or three twists and comes together to look like a short, twirled rope with no gaps. Tuck and pinch the ends slightly to join them and place on a prepared baking sheet. Repeat until you have used up all the dough.

Bake in the oven for 20 minutes, or until golden. These will be crunchy on the outside with a slight softness in the middle, but if you want a biscotti-style crunch, turn the oven down to 160°C (350°F/gas 4) and bake for 8 minutes longer, making sure they don't catch. Leave to cool on a wire rack.

YIAYIA ANGELIKI

Born Sparti, 1928

'I must have been making these for over 50 years. The kids would take them to the markets at school and sell them, they'd be the sell-outs every year. I can't even remember how many drachmas they must have sold them for. Probably the equivalent to a euro for a little bag of them. Then when the grandkids moved to England, I'd send them packages and packages of them.

I moved to Athens because we had so many problems of unrest in my village. We lived through the occupation of Germans and Italians, then even after the war, the *andartes* (Greek partisans) cleared us out of house and home. They took everything we had and didn't even leave a nail on the wall. They'd become used to only having themselves to answer to and some of them ended up turning against their own people. It was a hard time for Greece with so much civil unrest and we became refugees in a sense – we had to leave our home and come to Athens where it was safer.

Athens was so beautiful then. Ampelokipoi was like a village. There were fields and meadows everywhere and there were shepherds all around. Now the house I lived in no longer exists. They built apartment blocks over it. It's unrecognisable now, the Athens of my youth. You wouldn't believe how green it was.'

YIAYIA OLGA'S MELOMAKARONA
(HONEY BISCUITS) FROM THESSALY

Soft, oval, almost cakey biscuits dipped in honey syrup and topped with a sprinkling of crunchy walnuts, *melomakarona* are the ultimate Christmas sweet here in Greece. They're found in bakeries from Corfu to Kastellorizo, but because raw Thessalian honey is some of the nation's best produce, baking them here with Olga in the company of many of the region's beekeepers is a real treat.

We bake together under the dappled light of an oak tree on one of the first good days of spring. She's quite young as grandmothers go, but she already has four grandchildren (on account of her marrying at the age of 19) and one of them is with her, clinging desperately to her leg.

We're in Yiayia Katina's (see page 147) garden and what seems like the whole village has turned up for this demonstration. Everyone finds it hilarious that we're cooking up a Christmas biscuit (cookie), spiked with cloves and cinnamon, on a day that the thermometer hits 35°C (95°F) but I don't mind. I could eat *melomakarona* all year round.

We eat them hot out of the oven, but with a twist: vanilla ice cream. Purists will say it's all wrong, but even Yiayia Olga and Yiayia Katina give it the thumbs up. The ice cream cuts through the sweetness of the honey and who can deny a hot-out-of-the-oven biscuit and ice-cream combo?

Makes 40 biscuits
Vegetarian

290 ml (9¾ fl oz/scant 1¼ cups) corn oil, plus extra for greasing
80 ml (2¾ fl oz/⅓ cup) cognac
90 g (3¼ oz/¾ cup) icing (confectioner's) sugar
zest of 2 oranges
70 ml (2¼ fl oz/generous ¼ cup) orange juice (about 2–3 oranges)
20 g (¾ oz/5 teaspoons) baking powder
1 teaspoon bicarbonate of soda (baking soda)
1 teaspoon ground cloves
1 teaspoon ground cinnamon
700 g (1 lb 9 oz/generous 5½ cups) plain (all-purpose) flour
350 g (12 oz/1½ cups) caster (superfine) sugar
650 g (1 lb 7 oz/generous 1¾ cups) good-quality honey (Yiayia Olga uses Odysea)
500 ml (17 fl oz/2 cups) water
2 small cinnamon sticks
50 g (2 oz/scant ½ cup) chopped walnuts

Preheat the oven to 200°C (425°F/gas 7) and grease a large baking sheet.

In a large bowl, combine the oil, cognac, icing sugar, orange zest and juice, baking powder, bicarbonate of soda and spices. Next, gradually whisk in the flour (Yiayia Olga uses her hand as a whisk).

Bring the mixture together, then work for a few minutes with your hands to ensure all the ingredients are combined into a thick, paste-like dough.

Grease a large oven tray or two depending on size with a splash of corn oil, then begin to mould the *melomakarona* by taking a lump of the mixture with a large spoon, rolling it into an oval shape in your hands and flattening it ever so lightly (minimum 1 cm/½ inch thickness). Then take a grater and press it into the dough with the fine side, leaving a bumpy texture on top for the honey and walnuts to cling onto. Place onto the prepared baking sheet and repeat until you've used all the dough.

Bake the biscuits in the oven for 15–20 minutes, checking on them after 10 minutes and again after 15 minutes. Once they've risen and are nicely browned, remove from the oven. You want them to be just a little bit squidgy in the middle – between a biscuit and a cake. Leave to cool.

Meanwhile, make the syrup. In a large saucepan, combine the sugar, honey and water. Bring to the boil over a medium heat. After a few minutes it should begin to bubble and foam. Reduce the heat and gently simmer, using a spoon to scoop off the foam.

Add the cinnamon sticks and simmer for a further 10 minutes. You don't want a very thick syrup but a light, golden consistency.

Once the *melomakarona* have cooled, pour the syrup over them using a ladle. Yiayia Olga uses all of hers and turns the *melomakarona* over in the syrup mix so that base and top are soaked through. You can add as much syrup as you like, depending on how much honey you can handle. Sprinkle over the chopped walnuts.

These will keep in an airtight container for a week, be it Christmas or any other time of year.

YIAYIA OLGA

Born Thessaly, 1963

'We would never, ever, ever consider making these at any time other than Christmas. Not even on an autumn or winter's day. *Melomakarona* are strictly seasonal and they conjure images of Christmas here in the village for me.

We might not be a lot of people living here now, but we still hold onto traditions. At Christmas, even since I was a little girl, children go door to door and sing the *kalanda* (carols), often carrying a triangle that they chime along with. *Melomakarona* are something we might give them as a treat for their efforts.'

YIAYIA SOFIA'S OLIVE OIL CAKE FROM CORFU

Born 1941, Corfu

Dedication by George Dafnis, olive oil producer at The Governor olive oil

Yiayia Sofia was the daughter of an olive producer. Our family's was the first olive mill with mill stones on the island. She didn't ever go to school but instead spent her winters picking olives and the summers working the other harvests, for example corn. At the time, even girls would work out on the land from ten years old. The olive harvesting method was really different back then. Yiayia would tell me about how she had to climb up into the trees from branch to branch and would whack the branches so that the olives would fall, to be picked by those waiting below.

Yiayia and I had so many arguments, but we'd always find a solution. We were both very stubborn, but for us to make up, she'd always make me food. One dish was chips (fries) but not the savoury kind. They were served with sugar, honey and sesame seeds – and fried in olive oil. The recipe I've chosen to share, though, is her olive oil cake recipe. I think people might appreciate that one more.

Serves 8–12
Vegetarian

130 g (4½ oz) Greek yoghurt
200 g (7 oz) whole eggs (from about 4 medium eggs)
150 g (5 oz/generous ⅔ cup) granulated sugar
150 ml (5 fl oz/scant ⅔ cup) extra virgin olive oil, plus extra for greasing
1 tablespoon vanilla extract
zest of 1 orange
200 g (7 oz/1⅔ cups) self-raising (self-rising) flour
pinch of salt
honey and chopped nuts, to serve

Preheat the oven to 180°C (400°F/gas 6) and grease a 8-inch (20 cm) cake tin (pan).

In a bowl, whisk together the yoghurt, eggs, sugar, olive oil, vanilla extract and orange zest.

Fold in the flour and salt, then pour the mixture into the prepared cake tin and bake for 40–50 minutes until it comes away from the sides and is golden on top, checking on it occasionally to make sure it doesn't get too brown.

Remove from the oven and allow to cool, then drizzle with a little honey and sprinkle with chopped nuts to serve.

YIAYIA ANASTASIA'S SIKOPITES
(FIG PIES) FROM CORFU

By September, the fig tree in my garden hangs so heavy with thick purple fruit that Yiayia and I start inviting the neighbours owning the adjoining bits of land to help themselves. At this point in the year you can usually find me rustling around at the top of the fig tree, Yiayia below pointing out which branches bear the best fruit.

We have different opinions on how best to use our bounty. I like a quick and easy fig jam. Yiayia turns her nose up at this, preferring her September *sikopita* ritual. She spends weeks making *sikopites* or *sikomagida* (literally translated to 'fig magic').

Packed with spices, *sikopites* are oval shaped 'pies' made from sun-dried figs and spiked with plenty of ouzo. They're perfect for chopping into yoghurt in the mornings, taking on long hikes or simply enjoying in the mid-morning with a Greek coffee.

Nothing can be more indicative of the time Yiayia pours into her food than the *sikopites* she makes at the end of summer. She dries her figs out for a week under her old bridal tulle before soaking them in ouzo and eventually wrapping them in fig leaves to be enjoyed throughout the year. Since I was a young girl, I've observed the long and drawn-out process of making this Corfiot delicacy. Yiayia's been known to keep her *sikopites* for up to a year, wrapped in fig leaves and hanging in the tulle, waiting for the right occasion to be sliced into and enjoyed with an iced ouzo.

Yiayia serves these to guests who come over for a coffee or an ouzo, but I sometimes like to add them to my cooking, chopping one up and incorporating it in a rice pilaf with lots of herbs, or adding the odd chunk or two to a pot of meatballs and sauce for a note of something sweet.

Makes around 6 pies
Vegan

2 kg (4 lb 8 oz) figs
1 litre (34 fl oz/4 cups) ouzo
2 tablespoons ground black pepper
1 tablespoon ground fennel seeds
1 tablespoon ground cinnamon
fig leaves, for wrapping the
    sikopites

Prepare the figs by cutting a cross incision at the top of each one and opening its inner flesh out. Place the figs on a large tray or board and leave to dry in the sun for a week under a fine tulle. Alternatively (and much to Yiayia's displeasure), bake in a fan oven at 100°C (225°F/gas ¼) for 6 hours.

Chop the dried figs into 1 cm (½ inch) cubes and place them in a bowl, then pour over the ouzo and leave them to soak overnight.

The next day, the figs should be soft. Add the spices and knead the figs, using your knuckles to press the mixture together and combine the ingredients.

When the mixture is combined and feels nice and malleable, take 3–4 heaped tablespoons of it and roll it into a ball between your palms. Flatten the ball slightly so that it looks like a thick burger patty. Repeat the process until you've used up all the mixture.

Preheat the oven to as low as it will go (ideally 50°C/125°F).

Wrap your sikopites in fig leaves. Place a fig leaf on the bottom, one on the top and use twine to tie them in place. Bake in the oven for 2 hours.

YIAYIA MARIA'S AMIGDALOPITA (ALMOND CAKE) FROM SIFNOS

A net curtain peels back to reveal a wisened old lady with a halo of white hair around a smiling face. I've ridden on the back of a scooter to get to Maria's, down bright whitewashed alleys that make my eyes ache. She lives next to her son's *kafeneion* in Sifnos, where tourists come thinking they're getting an authentic experience without knowing that a quirky home full of ancient crockery, family photos, crochet and this yiayia, the real picture of Sifnian life, sits metres away from them.

Together we make an *amigdalopita*, which is essentially an almond cake. Thanks to the syrup and to the quantity of eggs, this is an incredibly moist dessert that is best enjoyed with a dollop of yoghurt or ice cream to cut through all the sugar. She's handwritten her recipe and tells me that baking is all about precision (though she does admit to adding and taking away on occasion and proudly concludes that regardless of this, her desserts always turn out well).

I'm shocked to read the recipe calls for 13 eggs, but she assures me it's on account of the enormous baking tray (pan) she uses. She used to supply the *kafeneion* with its desserts and her almond cake recipe was always a stand-out, so she's used to making vast quantities. I've halved the recipe to fit a smaller tray.

Serves 12
Vegetarian

6 large eggs, separated
250 g (9 oz/1 cup plus 4 teaspoons) caster (superfine) sugar
½ heaped teaspoon ground cinnamon
pinch of salt
115 g (4 oz/scant 1¼ cups) ground almonds (almond meal)
35 g (1¼ oz/⅓ cup) dried breadcrumbs, blitzed
1 heaped teaspoon baking powder
50 ml (1¾ fl oz/3 tablespoons) cognac

FOR THE SYRUP

140 g (4¾ oz/scant ⅔ cup) granulated sugar
130 ml (4½ fl oz/generous ½ cup) water
½ slice of lemon

Preheat the oven to 170°C (375°F/gas 5) and grease and line a 23 cm (9 inch) brownie tin with baking parchment.

In a bowl, combine the egg yolks with the sugar, cinnamon and salt. Yiayia Maria uses her hand like a giant whisk, but you can use a wooden spoon. Once combined, fold in the almonds and breadcrumbs.

In a separate bowl, use an electric whisk on high speed to beat the egg whites until fluffy, frothy, soft peaks – about 4 minutes.

Working quickly, so as not to leave your fluffy whites too long, dissolve the baking powder into the cognac, then pour this into the yolk mixture, stirring to combine.

Spoon a little of the egg white into the yolk mixture and thoroughly stir to loosen the mixture. Then gradually and gently fold the rest of the egg whites into the yolk and almond mixture.

Transfer the finished batter into the prepared tin and bake for 25 minutes, or until risen and deeply golden on top, and a skewer insterted into the middle comes out clean.

Meanwhile, make the syrup by combining all the ingredients in a saucepan, bringing them to the boil, then simmering over a medium heat for 15 minutes.

Pour the syrup onto the cake as soon as it's out of the oven, letting it seep into it. Leave to cool before cutting into squares and serving.

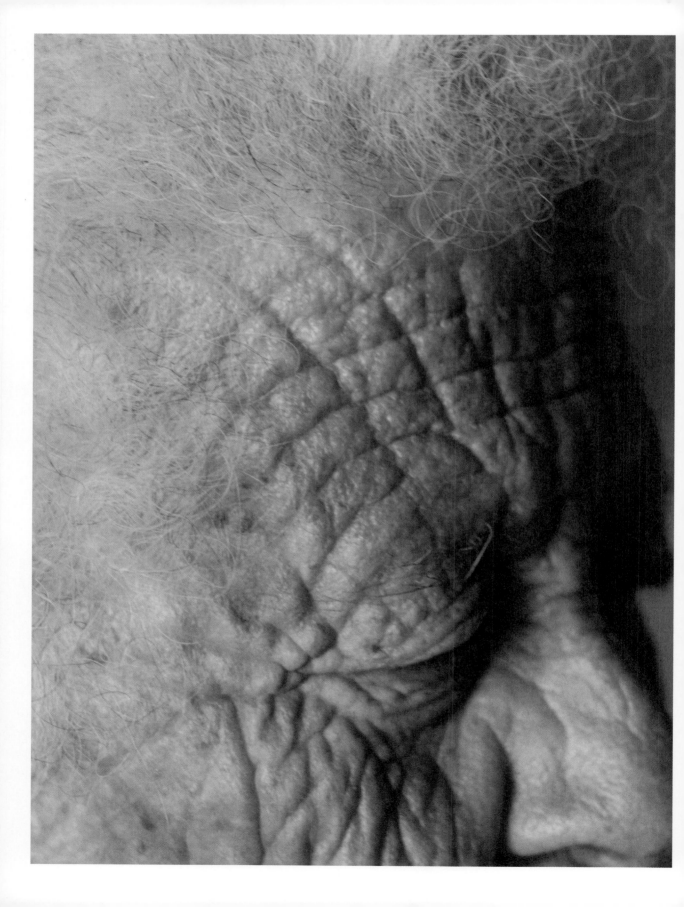

YIAYIA MARIA

Born Sifnos, 1941

'Here on Sifnos so many of us share the same name – including our surnames – that each family has its own nickname out of necessity. I'm not sure where mine, Patsoulenia, came from, but it was the name of my great aunt (the sister of my grandmother). She took care of me because my mother and father had five children and we were all too much for her to look after. I was the only one of my siblings who was sent off to live with her in the village. I never understood why they chose me, because I was the second child, not the youngest.

I had to have a lot of patience living with her because she wasn't of my mother's generation, she was of my yiayia's generation. She was incredibly strict, and I had a hard time with her. She had worked in Egypt for many years for other families and when she came back to Sifnos, my mum and dad thought it best to let her raise me. If there's anything I've learned in life, it's to have patience with other people. Otherwise, you just can't get by. You get too wound up within yourself.

I only went to primary school because there wasn't a secondary school close to my village and my parents didn't have the means to send me. We were behind in a lot of things for many years here on the island. I was born during the German occupation and for many years after it we didn't have any of the modern luxuries that other people did. There was only one doctor on the island and even he was barely ever at his home when we would go knocking. If you had a problem, he'd be annoyed that you were keeping him from going fishing.

My great aunt taught me how to do a lot of things, one of which was to cook, and I appreciate her for that. This *amigdalopita* is one I would always be asked to make for weddings. We have lots of desserts that feature almonds on the island and traditionally, it's these desserts that we serve at weddings. I'd also make six or seven trays of these for the Assumption of Mary on 15 August or at Easter. It always goes down well, and I have no idea how to make it for any fewer than ten people.'

KYRIA RITA'S WHIPPED YOGHURT WITH ORANGE BLOSSOM, STRAWBERRIES AND CANDIED PISTACHIOS FROM ANDROS

Dedication by Allegra Pomilio, founder and art director at Mèlisses, Andros

There is a place in the village of Paleopoli very dear to me: a small *periptero* (kiosk), where the owner, Kyria Rita, serves the most hearty, delicious meals. The entire village adores her and in true Greek island fashion, she knows everyone and everyone knows her.

I love to hike in the area in late spring and stop there for a quick but wholesome lunch. I always order a classic *fourtalia* omelette with mint and local sausage, followed by Greek salad and the most delicious selection of homemade spoon sweets. Everything is, of course, cooked to perfection.

Rita's house, situated just above the periptero, has the lushest and most verdant garden on the island, where she grows fruit and citrus trees. Spoon sweets are a Greek delicacy, but hers are sublime. The most special and refined one is made with lemon blossoms, which was an absolute revelation to me and has inspired many of my desserts at Mèlisses, including this one.

I love to serve the macerated strawberries and blossoms on a pillowy layer of whipped Greek yoghurt, combining the velvety texture and floral scent, which reminds me of the spoon sweets she serves with creamy yoghurt.

This is the perfect recipe for a last-minute dessert as it requires only a few elements, however, it's important to choose the highest-quality ingredients you can find. We love to serve this at Easter day lunch, followed by freshly baked *tsoureki*. Topped with lemony, crunchy pistachios, it is our favourite spring dessert at Mèlisses.

Serves 5–6
Vegetarian

FOR THE MACERATED STRAWBERRIES
250 g (9 oz) strawberries , hulled and quartered
1 tablespoon caster (superfine) sugar
handful of fresh orange/lemon blossom flowers (if you can't find them, you can replace them with 1 tablespoon orange blossom water)
juice of ½ lemon
small handful of fresh mint leaves

FOR THE CARAMELISED PISTACHIOS
50 g (2 oz/scant ¼ cup) caster (superfine) sugar
50 g (2 oz/⅓ cup) shelled roasted pistachios
pinch of salt

FOR THE WHIPPED YOGHURT
200 ml (7 fl oz/scant 1 cup) whipping cream
200 g (7 oz) Greek yoghurt (minimum 5% fat)
1 tablespoon honey
6 drops orange blossom water
zest and juice of 1 lemon
zest of 1 orange

Put the strawberries in a bowl and add the sugar, lemon or orange blossoms, lemon juice and mint leaves, and stir to coat. Cover the bowl and refrigerate for 1 hour, allowing the berries to macerate.

For the caramelised pistachios, place the sugar in a small saucepan over a low heat and heat until you have a beautiful amber-gold caramel. Remove the pan from the heat and add the roasted pistachios and salt. Mix with a spatula, ensuring that the pistachios are coated with the caramel. Transfer the caramelised pistachios to a sheet of baking parchment and use a whole lemon to roll them out until evenly distributed (the lemon won't stick to the caramel, allowing the nuts to be distributed across the sheet of paper, and will also infuse them with its essential oils). Leave the pistachios to cool completely, then roughly chop with a knife.

Right before serving, whip the cream until it is just holding its shape (about halfway whipped), then add the yoghurt, followed by the honey, orange blossom water, lemon juice and lemon and orange zest, then keep whipping until it reaches a soft, pillowy texture.

Assemble the dessert by placing a generous spoon of the whipped yoghurt in small individual bowls, top with the strawberries and their syrup (make sure to discard the lemon or orange blossoms if you used them) and finish with the chopped caramelised pistachios.

ANNA'S ROSE SPOON SWEET FROM ASIA MINOR

Glyko tou koutaliou or 'spoon sweet' is what Anna is famous for in Andros. Not strictly a yiayia, but a mother of two and an inspiring matriarch all the same, Anna is someone I absolutely couldn't leave out of this book. I first cooked with her when I stayed at my favourite spot in Andros, the foodie outpost Mèlisses, and I've been a long-time admirer of her preserved fruits ever since.

Spoon sweets are what you might be given at the end of your meal in a Cycladic taverna. Owing to the abundance of fruit on Andros, the greenest of all the Cycladic islands, these sweets are made in most homes here. At Mèlisses, I first ate Anna's rose petal spoon sweet on yoghurt for breakfast and was instantly transported over the waters of the Aegean further east, to places with domed roofs we Greeks can no longer pronounce; to the Turkish delight we now call *loukoumi* and to a past that is just as much a part of Andros's history as it is Istanbul's.

Anna sips a Greek coffee in her rose garden as she explains that this dish – inspired by her mother-in-law, Yiayia Marta, who inherited the recipe from her own yiayia – isn't 'Andriotiki' after all. It hails from Asia Minor, where Yiayia Marta's yiayia came from. I love to linger on the notion that a refugee brought this magic recipe to Andros and Anna, a refugee to Greece herself, would be the one to preserve its memory and serve it to people visiting the island from all corners of the globe.

It is sweet. It is rich. It is beautiful spooned on top of ice cream or Greek yoghurt, shining ruby red. It's also special, in that only those with fresh, fragrant rose petals in their vicinity can make it.

Makes 2–3 small jars
Vegetarian

300 g (10½ oz) edible, fragrant pink or red rose petals, washed and the bottom part of the petal that meets the stem sliced off
800 g (1 lb 12 oz/3⅔ cups) granulated sugar
300 ml (10 fl oz/1¼ cups) water
1 heaped tablespoon honey
juice of ½ lemon

On a tray, rub a couple of handfuls of the rose petals with a handful of the sugar. Crush and squeeze the petals in your palms as you go and keep adding more petals and sugar into the tray as you go along, until you have used up all the petals and half the sugar.

The petals should release some moisture into the tray. You want that, so don't be tempted to drain it away. Transfer the sugared petals to an airtight container and refrigerate overnight.

The next day, transfer the petals and juices a large saucepan and tip in the remaining sugar and the water, then bring to the boil, stirring with a wooden spoon and a wooden spoon only (as per Anna's instruction!).

Once bubbling away, reduce the heat to medium and simmer for 20 minutes, then remove from the heat. Cover and infuse overnight.

The next day (or at least 8 hours later), preheat the oven to 150°C (325°F/gas 3) and sterilise your jars for 10 minutes. While they sterilise, bring the rose and sugar mixture to the boil again and simmer over a medium heat for 10 minutes. Anna swears by the double-simmer method to ensure the spoon sweet is nice and thick.

Finally, add the honey and lemon, then fill the jars and turn upside down to secure their caps. These will last 6 months in your fridge.

ANNA

Born Albania, 1967

'When I first came to Greece I had to come by foot. We were illegally crossing into Greece from Albania and so had no option but to walk. We didn't have tents or sleeping bags or anything. We would just walk for as long as possible, then sleep on whatever dry ground we could find. There were times we had to make a run for it into the mountains at night, for fear of the police finding us. My brother had to pick me up and run with me on his back because I just couldn't make it.

Somewhere around Ioannina, it was February and freezing cold. We were crossing a big river and my brother said I shouldn't get in fully, that he'd carry me on his back. So we began crossing, but the current was so strong that he couldn't walk with me on his back. When I got down off his back in the middle of the river my feet didn't even touch the bottom and the current carried me away. I was waiting for death to come for me but somehow, someone found me on the riverbanks and pulled me out. I was only 23. I just burst into tears. I didn't even have a change of clothes with me.

When I first came to Greece, everyone told me to change my name to sound less Albanian, so my name became Anna from Suzanna. We were all scared of racism at the time, so we adapted. There was something about Andros when I first came here that called to me, though. I felt welcomed here on the island and the people here were so kind to me. There was something in the air here and it was in this very place that I became passionate about cooking.'

YIAYIA SEVASTI'S RIZOGALO
(RICE PUDDING) FROM RHODES

Yiayia Sevasti lives in Rhodes, the largest island in the Dodecanese and one with an impressive old town that sits within dramatic medieval fortifications. I'm reminded of Jerusalem here and can sense just how far east I am. Bazaars, the domed roofs of mosques and traditional hammams nod to our proximity to Turkey, while the arched doorways and wrought iron lit passageways of the old town are a vestige of the island's Venetian colonisers.

In the spirit of mixing cultures and heritage, Sevasti chooses to show me how to make her famous *rizogalo*. This rice pudding is not far from the Turkish *fırın sutlaç* and for good reason, it's a dessert that is incredibly common here in Rhodes, perhaps because of the island's proximity to Turkey. Sevasti also – quite uncharacteristically for her time – married a Sri Lankan man and proudly claims to be excellent at anything involving rice.

This one's rich, creamy and incredibly soul soothing eaten either hot or cold. Serve with a sprinkling of cinnamon or if you fancy being a little unorthodox, a shaving of cacao.

Serves 6
Vegetarian

1.25 (40 fl oz/4¾ cups) litres water
250 g glacé rice (or pudding rice), washed thoroughly
170 ml (5¾ fl oz/scant ¾ cup) single (light) cream
130 ml (4½ fl oz/generous ½ cup) condensed milk
75 ml (2½ fl oz/5 tablespoons) milk
60 g (2 oz) sugar
2 teaspoons vanilla extract

In a large saucepan, bring the water to the boil. Add the rice and cook, covered, over a medium-high heat for 20 minutes until the rice has thickened and soaked up the water. Give it a stir every once in a while to ensure the rice doesn't stick to the bottom of the pan.

Once thickened, reduce the heat to low simmer and add the cream and condensed milk.

In a separate bowl, mix the milk with the sugar and whisk until combined, then add the vanilla extract before stirring into the rice.

Cook for 10 minutes more. If it is still a bit on the runny side, turn up the heat. Keep stirring at this stage, as you don't want the rice to stick to the bottom and burn. Once the *rizogalo* is nice and thick, remove from the heat.

Serve hot or cold. It will keep in the refrigerator for up to 5 days.

YIAYIA SEVASTI

Born Symi, 1949

'I was married when I was 16 and my husband was pushing 30. I learned to cook when I was young because I married so young. My brother worked on ships and he loved me very much so he told me he'd get me married. That was the best thing to do for your sister at the time, find her a good man. I didn't really want to get married but that's what it was like in those times, the families arranged a good match for you. We called this kind of matchmaking a *proxenio*.

Anyway, my brother worked with this handsome sailor from Sri Lanka. One day he called me and told me to come to the port as his ship came in so that we could get a good look at this friend that he had lined up for me. He was very skinny, so he didn't look that much older than me. He didn't speak very much Greek either, but I didn't mind that. My father and my brother liked him and that was enough. All my family loved him and between us, love blossomed slowly but surely. It's been a long life together since then.'

YIAYIA SOFIA'S MILOPITAKIA
(MINI APPLE PIES) FROM KARPATHOS

Yiayia Sofia comes highly recommended by everyone I speak with in advance of arriving in Karpathos. She lives up an impossibly winding mountain pass, in the remote village of Olympos.

On the road up to Olympos, whole chunks of the mountain have fallen off the towering cliffs above and into the road. Clouds swirl ahead, encircling the village tucked into the mountainside, making it feel like an enchanted place straight out of a book of fairy tales.

Sofia is the first person I spot on my arrival, her bright blue eyes beaming as I tell her that I've been trying to reach her by phone for almost a month. With a little gentle persuasion, she agrees to show me how to make her famous *milopitakia*, a kind of sweet empanada of apples and walnuts – just the warming treat I want after the treacherous drive up here.

These are great to travel with, making for the ultimate dessert in a packed lunch or picnic. Or else eat hot out of the oven, with a scoop of vanilla ice cream.

Makes about 20 pies
Vegetarian

650 g (1 lb 7 oz) apples, peeled and chopped into small cubes
125 g (4 oz/generous ½ cup) granulated sugar
2 tablespoons ground cinnamon
75 g (2½ oz/⅔ cup) chopped walnuts
100 ml (3½ fl oz/scant ½ cup) freshly squeezed orange juice, plus extra as needed
100 ml (3½ fl oz/scant ½ cup) white wine
100 ml (3½ fl oz/scant ½ cup) sunflower oil
450 g (1 lb/3 ⅔ cups) self-raising (self-rising) flour, plus extra as needed
milk (any type), for brushing
1 heaped tablespoon mixed black and white sesame seeds

Preheat the oven to 180°C (400°F/gas 6) and line a baking sheet with baking parchment.

Combine the chopped apple, sugar, cinnamon and walnuts in a bowl, then transfer to a frying pan (skillet) and cook for 6–8 minutes over a medium heat until soft and sticky but the apples are still holding their shape. Remove from the heat and set aside to cool.

In a large bowl, combine the orange juice, wine and oil, then sift in the flour, bit by bit, stirring with a wooden spoon as you go. When the mixture becomes too stiff for the spoon, use your hands and begin to really knead the dough and work the remaining flour in. The dough should come together to be smooth, elastic and not sticky. If yours is too dry, add 1 teaspoon more orange juice at a time, kneading it in between additions to see if it has reached the right consistency. If it is too wet, do the same with teaspoons of flour. Sofia then bashes the hell out of the dough for a good 5 minutes, then leaves it to rest in the bowl for a further 10 minutes with a wet kitchen towel over it.

Once the dough has rested, very lightly flour your work surface, grab a walnut-size amount of the dough (you'll need around 30–35 g/1–1¼ oz per *milopita*), roll it into a ball, flatten slightly on the surface and then use a rolling pin to roll it out into a thin circle about 15–20 cm (6–8 inches) in diameter.

Add a tablespoon of the cooled apple mixture into the middle of the circle of dough, then fold over one side to meet the other side, creating a semi-circle. Use a pastry brush to spread a thin layer of milk on the dough where the two edges meet. Pinch the edges so that they join together well and wheel a pastry cutter around the curved edge. Place the *milopita* on the prepared baking sheet, stab a small hole in the centre to let the air escape when baking and repeat until you've used up all the dough.

Brush the top of each *milopita* with milk, then sprinkle over a few sesame seeds before baking the pies in the oven for 20 minutes, turning halfway through. Remove from the oven when the pastry is nicely golden. Serve while still slightly warm, with a cup of coffee.

YIAYIA SOFIA

Born Karpathos, 1952

'I've had my taverna, Mike's, for 40 years now. Before opening it in my twenties I'd worked at various small restaurants but I wanted to be my own boss so I took out a little loan and opened up my own place. At the time, my husband was away in America. He was gone for ten years. We didn't even have telephones here to talk to each other back then, so the only way we communicated was through letter writing. We didn't even have a proper road connecting the village with the rest of the island until the 1980s. If we really needed to, we had to walk to another part of Karpathos or go with a *kaiki* (fishing boat).

We're still very much separated in Olympos, even from the rest of Karpathos. Nowhere else on the island will you see people wearing our dress. The tradition was passed down to us from our mothers and grandmothers and we still make our own clothing. It's out of habit more than anything and I suppose up here, there's no pressure to change.'

YIAYIA ELENI'S HALVA
FROM KASTELLORIZO

One of Greece's most remote islands, the tiny Kastellorizo (population under 300 inhabitants) is so close to Turkey that the distance is swimmable and locals like Yiayia Eleni have been known to hop on a boat on market day to go over to the Turkish mainland for their weekly grocery shop. Quite organically, traditions and customs between East and West meld on an island like Kastellorizo, culinary influences included.

Halva, like many Greek dishes, has its origins much further east than Europe. Meaning 'sweet dish' in Arabic, this treat enjoyed in the Dodecanese is most likely to have made its way into Greece via Turkey. It crops up all over Greece when we enter *nistia*, the period of fasting before Easter, which requires the Christian Orthodox community to adopt 40 days of veganism before breaking the fast on Easter Sunday.

Where some *halva* is made with semolina and ground almonds to create a thick, sweet paste that can then be turned into a mould and sliced into, Yiayia Eleni in Kastellorizo likes to use flour for hers. She tells me she likes a denser Halva, especially when she's fasting. We make this together in Eleni's home that sits right on the harbour of Kastellorizo. Incidentally, the high-ceilinged home with its original dark wood beams and airy entrance belonged to Eleni's own yiayia, the woman behind this very recipe.

Serves 25
Vegan

200 g (7 oz) margarine
130 ml (4½ fl oz/generous ½ cup)
  olive oil
470 g (1 lb ¾ oz/2 cups plus
  2 tablespoons) granulated sugar
700 ml (24 fl oz/scant 3 cups)
  lukewarm water
300 g (10½ oz/scant 2½ cups)
  plain (all-purpose) flour
ground cloves and cinnamon,
  to serve

In a large, non-stick frying pan (skillet) melt the margarine with the olive oil over a medium heat.

In a separate bowl, mix together the sugar and water, stirring to combine until the sugar dissolves in the water, then set aside.

Once the margarine has melted in the pan, gradually stir in the flour, increasing the heat slightly but stirring constantly so that the flour doesn't burn. Keep stirring slowly for about 10 minutes until it takes on a nice, deep biscuit tone.

Add the water and sugar solution, increasing the heat to high, and cook for 5 minutes, or until the begins to thicken and bubble. Once it begins to come away easily from the pan onto your wooden spoon, the *halva* is ready.

Use a tablespoon to scoop the halva into small bite-size pieces and arrange on a plate or serving tray. Yiayia Eleni serves hers with a sprinkling of ground cloves and cinnamon.

YIAYIA ELENI

Born Kastellorizo, 1941

'Elsewhere they make *halva* with semolina, but we're a small island and we only have a certain amount of resources here so we were raised on *halva* made with flour. We would go over to Turkey to go to the bazaars every Friday. It made more sense because we're closer to the Turkish mainland than we are to Rhodes and there's a lot more produce to choose from there.

We had a lot more contact with the people opposite in the olden days before our nations were divided. My dad's family had houses over there. We exchanged recipes as well as customs. Here in Kastellorizo, when someone leaves for a long journey, we traditionally throw water behind them for good luck. They do that in Turkey, too.'

KYRIA PENELOPE'S PORTOKALOPITA (ORANGE PIE) FROM THE CYCLADES

For me, summer isn't summer without a stop off in Tinos. In recent years it's become an island known for its exceptional gastronomy and many of my favourite eating spots are situated on the island. One of these is O Megalos Kafenes. At the heart of Pyrgos, this *kafeneion* has been in the care of Penelope's family for the past century. I head there every morning for breakfast on my holiday. It is famous for its *galaktoboureko* (custard pastry dessert) but the sweet treat I'm always after here is a *portokalopita*.

More of a cake than a pie, though made with filo sheets, this moist, orange-spiked slice of Tinos is baked up daily for the *kafeneion* by Kyria Penelope. I arrive in time to watch her whip one up at such speed I barely have time to note down the recipe. While we wait for it to bake, Penelope strolls with us to the *kafeneion* to check they have enough desserts to see them through to tomorrow, greeting what feels like a hundred people in three minutes. The kafeneion has barely changed since she was a little girl, with the same, aged set of playing cards from her pappou residing in a wooden cabinet on the wall.

We eat our portokalopita outside the café, under an ancient plane tree. The only addition I make is to add a blob of yoghurt to cut through the sweetness of the syrup Penelope so generously douses it in.

Serves 8–12
Vegan

500 g (1 lb 2 oz) ready-made
  filo pastry
230 g (8¼ oz/1 cup plus
  1 tablespoon) granulated sugar
250 ml (8½ fl oz/1 cup) corn oil,
  plus extra for greasing
4 eggs
4 teaspoons baking powder
zest of 1 orange
250 g (9 oz) good-quality
  Greek yoghurt

FOR THE SYRUP

400 g (14 oz) sugar
750 ml (25 fl oz/3 cups) water
zest of 2 oranges

Dry out the filo by leaving the sheets in a baking tray (pan) for a day or out in the sun for a couple of hours.

Preheat the oven to 170°C (375°F/gas 5) and prepare a deep 34 x 26 cm (13½ x 10 inch) baking dish by greasing the sides and lining it with baking parchment.

In a bowl, whisk together the sugar, oil, eggs, baking powder and yoghurt with an electric whisk for 30 seconds until light and airy.

Crunch up the filo sheets. They should crisp and break apart into small pieces with very little effort. You want to break up the sheets by crushing them between your fingers. Aim for 1 cm (½ inch) pieces, but some may be even smaller – that's fine, as long as you have a mix of sizes for a light and airy texture.

Add the filo shards to the bowl of wet ingredients, ensuring all the filo is incorporated and using your hands to combine.

Pour the mixture into the prepared dish and bake for 30–50 minutes until it's nicely brown on top and a knife inserted into the middle comes out clean.

Meanwhile, make the syrup by combining all the ingredients in a saucepan and bringing to the boil, then reducing the heat and simmering for 15 minutes.

Remove the *portokalopita* from the oven and allow to cool in the tray, then pour over the syrup.

KYRIA PENELOPE

Born Tinos, 1955

'I'm the dessert supplier at the *kafeneion*. Whatever the day, I'm turning out *galaktoboureko* or portokalopita for the village. The *kafeneion* has always been in our family. My pappou and yiayia looked after it in the past and now it's been passed on to my son. In the 1920s my grandfather ran it. Then in the 1940s, my father, who was a fishmeran, had his *kaiki* boat sunk by the Germans during the occupation so he was left without work and took over from my pappou to work at the *kafeneion*.'

YIAYIA LIZA'S PASTA FROLLA FROM KEFALONIA

Yiayia Liza is a hidden treasure, one of those rare, magical creatures that seem completely removed from their setting, not belonging to the humble streets of Athens. She lives in a beautiful neoclassical home that's tucked into the graffiti-tagged streets of Exarcheia, a neighbourhood that for many years has been known for its anarchic leanings and has of late become a bit 'trendy'.

I step into her bright hallway, sun drenching through the glass ceiling and giving a sense of openness I don't expect of a downtown home. Liza, ruby red lippy perfectly applied, greets me, guiding me past canvases of art and a rich, Bordeaux-toned living room dotted with antiques, showing me into a large, leafy courtyard. Out on the wrought iron table, a tart, slick with apricot jam (jelly), is awaiting my arrival.

In Italy, *pasta frolla* is a sweet shortcrust pastry recipe that's often used for *crostata* or *torta della nonna* (grandmother's tart). Having made its way across the water to the Ionian, where Liza has her roots, *pasta frolla* has become the term we Greeks use for a jam tart. Between apron demonstrations and an ode to the electric whisk, Liza dances around her kitchen, showing me how easy it is to craft the perfect dessert for all seasons.

Serves 12–16
Vegetarian

250 g (9 oz) butter, at room temperature, cubed, plus extra for greasing
1 whole egg and 2 egg yolks
zest and juice of 1 orange
zest of 1 lemon
50 ml (1¾ fl oz/3 tablespoons) cognac
150g (5 oz) sugar
520 g (1 lb 2¾ oz/generous 4 cups) plain (all-purpose) flour, plus extra for dusting
400 g (14 oz) jam (jelly; Liza uses homemade apricot jam mixed with a dash of cognac)

Preheat the oven to 180°C (400°F/gas 6) and grease a 23 cm (9 inch) ceramic tart dish.

In a large bowl, beat the butter with an electric whisk until it's light and fluffy. Incorporate the egg and egg yolks, whisking for a further minute or so.

Next, work in the orange juice and zest, lemon zest, cognac and sugar, whisking until combined.

Now gradually add the flour, whisking as you go. You may want to change the whisks on the electric whisk to the dough hooks. Your aim is for quite a thick dough. Liza takes a little amount and makes a ball with it between her palms to check if it's good to go. If it rolls into a ball and retains its shape, then you can move on to the next step.

Take half of the dough and spread it across the base of the prepared tart dish, pressing lightly with your fingertips to even out the bottom layer, then spread the jam over the top with a spoon or spatula, taking care to spread it out across the base in an even layer.

Next, make the lattice top for the tart. Take a large-ish piece of the remaining dough and roll it out on a lightly floured surface into a sausage shape that's long enough fit around the perimeter of the tart dish. Press it into the sides of the dish to create a crust, lightly placing it over the jam without pushing it too far in.

Now use the rest of the dough to create sausages that will criss-cross over the tart. Liza rolls out about 11 long sausage shapes, placing the first across the middle and then adding the others to either side, then across to create a lattice effect. You might decide you want thicker pieces or thinner, depending on if you prefer more pastry or more jam in your tart.

Once topped, bake the tart in the oven for 35–45 minutes, or until golden brown on top.

YIAYIA LIZA

Born Athens, 1939

'Since I was married, we would go to our summer house in Kefalonia. There were many yiayiades there who had fantastic recipes and it was one of these ladies that gave me my recipe for *pasta frolla*. Funnily enough, people in Greece tend to call this dessert *pasta flora*, but those from the Ionian Islands will know that the correct term is *pasta frolla*, from the Italian influence on our islands.

In 1953 we had awful earthquakes in the Ionian. Zakynthos and Kefalonia had a terrible time of it, but thankfully, Corfu with its beautiful old town was spared. My great-grandmother's house in Kefalonia was devastated. The bottom half of the house was still intact, and it became the foundation for our own home and renovation. When we began restoring it in the 1960s it was an absolute nightmare. There was no electricity in the village. Can you imagine? Back then it was a nine-hour boat from Piraeus to get to Kefalonia – even getting there took some determination.

Many Greeks in Athens have second homes somewhere on an island or along the coast. The city empties out in the hot summer months. The house in Kefalonia is really where I have loved to host all my life. Every Easter around 20 of us gather there and I do everything for the family. I'm an artist and spend the entire year painting, but in the summer I take time out to be in Kefalonia and I turn my hand to my other art, cooking.'

YIAYIA (AND!) ANASTASIA'S CHERRY PLUM JAM FROM CORFU

Yiayia has never much been one for desserts, but our trees are so heavy with fruit every summer that she's had to resign herself (or me) to bubbling up a jam (jelly) or two when the branches of the trees around the house begin to droop. This recipe is perhaps the only one Yiayia and I have ever come up with together. Each July we have an abundance of cherry plums in various shades of red and purple and Yiayia tasks me with making a jam, then swiftly takes over and tells me exactly what to do, shoving me out of the way of the pot of boiling fruit. My contribution is the basil, which Yiayia grows outside of her little whitewashed house but never seems to use in her food. It adds a gentle perfume to the jam that sings of summer on the island.

Makes 3 small jars
Vegetarian

2.5 kg (5lb 10 oz) cherry plums, stoned
800 g (1 lb 12 oz/3⅔ cups) sugar
2 tablespoons good-quality honey
5 basil leaves, finely chopped

Combine the plums with the sugar and honey in a large saucepan and bring to the boil before reducing the heat and simmering for 2 hours until thickened. When it's almost ready, stir in the basil.

Pour into sterilised jars (see page 222) then turn the jars upside down to secure their lids.

YIAYIA ANASTASIA

Born Corfu, 1937

'I did go to school once, but it didn't last very long. They tried to send me to night school because in the day my family needed me to work out on the land. Corfu was an agricultural island before it was an island for tourism. Poor families like mine couldn't afford to have a single child that didn't pull their weight.

I was out working the land since the age of seven, long days in the sweltering sun. Real work. Then there was a rule brought in that children in Greece had to attend some form of education. I didn't last long at night school. By the time my day of work had finished, I was exhausted and didn't have the *kefi* (desire) to go.

It all came to a head when the teacher singled me out in front of the whole class to read something out loud from the blackboard. She came and stood next to my desk and kept demanding that I read what she'd written but the problem was, I didn't know how to. I'd never learned. I'm not sure what was going through my mind but in that moment under pressure, I bit her hand in front of everyone and then ran out of the room and all the way home.'

THANK YOUS

Writing a book like this is not a solitary task. *Yiayia* was made possible because of so many extra hands lent in the research phase. Organising Greek grandmas that are used to saying 'Yes, just come and we'll talk about it on the day', is no easy feat. Thank you to the grandchildren, family members and loved ones of the women featured in this book. Without your powers of persuasion, the homes you opened up to us and the beds you made for us in those homes, it might have never happened.

My biggest collaborator in this project has been Marco Arguello, a good friend and incredibly talented photographer who made travelling while pregnant feel (for the most part) effortless and fun. Thank you for the beautiful photos but also for your humour, stamina and ability to make light of even the most taxing situations. Chasing goats, cattle and Snickers ice cream as well as yiayiades across Greece with you are fond memories I will treasure. I'll never forget those crazy months and the commitment you gave to such a busy schedule. It means a lot.

Second to Marco, Jasmine Phillips, recipe tester extraordinaire, has saved my life, taking on the task of testing the recipes for a reader beyond Greece. Your diligence and focus on the details will make this a much better book than I could have hoped to have written without you.

In the pages of this book are recipes generously shared by fellow Greek foodies along with heartfelt dedications to their own Yiayiades. Thank you for the time it took you all to do this. It makes this book even more precious.

Huge appreciation also to the Society of Authors and K Blundell Trust, whose generous grant went into powering my latest granny mission. I've felt so looked after since joining the society. Thank you.

This book would not have come to fruition were it not for my agents at The Blair Partnership who saw promise in my cooking with grandmothers brand, Matriarch Eats. They have held my hand after a rocky introduction to the world of publishing and have restored my faith in the industry since I signed with them at the start of this journey.

The same can be said for the team at Hardie Grant, who have been understanding with my pressured pregnancy schedule. It helps that on finding your book has been commissioned in the same week that you see two blue lines, your editors are also pregnant with their first babies. Glory be to matriarchs!

Founder of the Matriarch Eats brand, Anastasia Miari has been cooking with and interviewing the world's grandmothers for six years. She holds a Guild of Food Writer's Award for 'inspired storytelling and great journalistic integrity'. She freelances for Lonely Planet Guides, *Monocle* Magazine, *Konfekt* Magazine, the *Guardian*, the *Sunday Times* and is *Courier* magazine's Athens-based correspondent. Anastasia is also the author of *Grand Dishes*, a book of stories and recipes from grandmothers of the globe inspired by her own Greek grandmother (Unbound, 2021).

@matriarcheats

INDEX

Quadrille, Penguin Random House UK, One Embassy Gardens,
8 Viaduct Gardens, London SW11 7BW

Quadrille Publishing Limited is part of the Penguin Random House group of companies
whose addresses can be found at global.penguinrandomhouse.com

Penguin
Random House
UK

Copyright text © Anastasia Miari 2023
Copyright photography © Marco Arguello 2023*

*Except:
Pages 16, 41–44 © Myrto Karagiannidou
Pages 31 (left), 111, 113 (portrait), 151, 152, 191–193, 212 © Anastasia Perahia
Pages 93, 115–117 © Eftihia Stefandi

Anastasia Miari has asserted her right to be identified as the author of this Work
in accordance with the Copyright, Designs and Patents Act 1988

No part of this book may be used or reproduced in any manner for the purpose of training artificial
intelligence technologies or systems. In accordance with Article 4(3) of the DSM Directive 2019/790,
Penguin Random House expressly reserves this work from the text and data mining exception.

First published by Hardie Grant Books in 2023

www.penguin.co.uk

A CIP catalogue record for this book is available from the British Library

Yiayia
ISBN: 978-178488-612-7

10 9 8 7 6

Publishing Director: Kajal Mistry
Acting Publishing Director: Emma Hopkin
Commissioning Editor: Eve Marleau
Editor: Isabel Gonzalez-Prendergast
Copy Editor: Lucy Kingett
Proofread: Vicky Orchard
Designer: Daniel New
Photographer: Marco Arguello
Production Controller: Sabeena Atchia

Colour reproduction by p2d
Printed in China by C&C Offset Printing Co., Ltd.

The authorised representative in the EEA is Penguin Random House Ireland,
Morrison Chambers, 32 Nassau Street, Dublin D02 YH68.

Penguin Random House is committed to a sustainable future for our business, our readers
and our planet. This book is made from Forest Stewardship Council® certified paper.

MIX
Paper | Supporting
responsible forestry
FSC® C018179